Improve Your Dressmaking

Previous books by the author
Dressmaking with Basic Patterns
Children's Wardrobe (BBC Publications)

Improve Your Dressmaking

Ann Ladbury

B.T. Batsford Ltd   London

ISBN 0 7134 0031 5
Filmset in Photina by
Servis Filmsetting Limited, Manchester

Printed in Great Britain
by The Anchor Press Ltd, Tiptree, Essex
for the publishers B.T. Batsford Limited
4 Fitzhardinge Street, London W1H 0AH

Contents

Introduction	7
Terms and equipment	9
Tailoring terms	9
Pressing equipment	12
Making up a garment	13
Darts	14
Pleats	15
Knife pleats	15
Inverted pleats	16
Box pleats	17
Pockets	19
Patch pockets	20
Flap pockets	21
Jetted pockets	22
Inside breast pocket	25
Trouser back pocket	25
Flap and jetted pockets	25
Welt pocket	26
Seam pockets	28
Men's side-seam trouser pockets	28
Interfacing	30
Interfacing a coat or jacket	30
Interfacing the back neck	32
Combined facings	33
Seams	35
Angled seam	35
Corded seam	35
Machine fell seam	37
Piped seam	37
Coat shoulder seam	39
Slot Seam	39
Welt seam	40
Reinforced trouser seams	41
Trouser creases	42
Linings	43
Loose linings	43
Lining a coat or jacket	45
Sleeve linings	47
Mounting	49
Shoulders	50
Shoulder pads	50
Sleeve head roll	51
Zip openings	52
Inserting a zip fastener	52
Man's trouser zip	55
Waistlines	59
Waistband backing	61
Waistline stay	61
Collars	62
Tailored coat or jacket collar	62
Semi-tailored coat or dress collar	66
Shirt collar	68
Sleeve openings	70
Seam opening	70
Gap-in-sleeve opening	70
Hemmed opening	70
Faced slit opening	71
Continuous strip opening	71
Shirt sleeve opening	72
Man's shirt sleeve opening	72
Cuffs	74
Wrap cuff	74
Dress cuff	74
Shirt cuff	75
Man's shirt cuff	76
Hole-and-button cuff	77
Tailored hole-and-button cuff	77
Hems	80
Narrow machined hem	80

Narrow hand-finished hem   80
Narrow hand-rolled hem   80
Wide straight hem   81
Curved hem   81
Circular hem   81
Coat hem   82
Reinforcing hems   83
Binding   **84**
Making crossway and bias strips   84
Single binding   85
Double binding   87
Flat binding   87
Fastenings   **89**
Worked buttonholes   89
Button snaps   91
Frogs and ball buttons   91
Hooks, eyes and bars   92
Men's trouser hooks   94
Press studs   94
Rouleau loops   95
Eyelets   98
Belts   **99**
Fabric belts   99
Belt loops   101
Fastening a belt   102
Finishing touches   **102**
Coat hangers   103
Swelled edge   103
Saddle stitching   103
Braids and lace   104
Top stitching   106
Fringes   107
Loop stitch finish   107
Shirring with elastic thread   108
Gauging   108
Cord gathering   108
Decorative facing   109
List of suppliers   **111**
Index   **112**

Acknowledgment

Many readers will know that I owe my life-long passion for sewing to my father. He was a master-tailor of the old school of perfectionists. He and his brothers were taught by my grandfather, a happy Austrian who came to this country at the end of the last Century. Already the master of superb European techniques, my grandfather also taught my grandmother, a down-to-earth Londoner, and many of her relations.

My father therefore had a wealth of experience and knowledge and when I was commissioned to write this book I asked him for his help with the techniques involved in making men's clothes. Sadly, he died suddenly, still sewing to perfection, the week before we were due to begin collaborating. Apart from being an indescribable blow to me personally, it left me with a practical problem. This I solved by unpicking one of my father's suits and writing about the construction as it came to pieces. I came across details which obviously only applied to particular figures and certain types of cloth so I have only included general information.

My father had started to teach men's tailoring to my friend Jean Holmes and I am grateful for her help with those sections. My thanks also go to Mary Peacock for the drawings, and to Jil Shipley for the finished artwork.

Introduction

This book caters for the home dressmaker who has mastered the basic skills and processes of making garments, and now wishes to tackle something more ambitious such as pockets, decorative seams and edging, tailored collars and cuffs, linings, and even men's shirts and trousers.

This is not intended to be a comprehensive book of advanced tailoring techniques; instead it is designed to show dressmakers at the intermediate stage how to deal with those advanced processes which are likely to arise and present problems. Many of the tips and information given on this section of processes can be applied to other areas of sewing.

A few fairly basic techniques have been included, such as setting in sleeves, making piped buttonholes, inserting zips and constructing cuffs, because these features occur frequently in dressmaking and it is handy to have all the information needed for making up a garment in one book. In addition, even the experienced dressmaker, who has been working these processes for years, may discover a few more useful tips.

Terms and Equipment

All dressmakers will be familiar with the terms and equipment in general use, but when tackling tailored garments and the fabrics associated with them, it helps to know the terms used by professional tailors, and to obtain some specialist items in addition to the usual needlework tools and materials. When making coats and jackets, for example, better results are achieved by using the correct haberdashery and linings. Using the proper equipment for the work in hand will always give a more professional finish.

Since specialist equipment may not be available at the local haberdashery store, a list of suppliers is provided at the end of this book from which one may obtain goods by mail order.

Tailoring terms

Bar tack or french tack
This is a bar of several threads about 3 mm or 5 mm ($\frac{1}{8}$ or $\frac{3}{16}$ in) long, covered with close loop stitch. It is usually made loose to attach linings at hems and seams, but it can also be used flat to strengthen pocket openings by sewing through all the layers and making small over-stitches instead of close loop stitch.

Basting
Basting is the term used by dressmakers to describe rows of large diagonal stitching. As a term used by tailors, it describes all forms of tacking (the stitch made to join material together temporarily). A 'baste' is a coat assembled for a fitting.

Beeswax
Small cakes of hard beeswax are used for coating threads for hand-sewing and sewing on buttons. It helps to strengthen the thread, and, when it is applied to a double thread, it causes the two threads to stick together and makes the sewing easier.

Betweens
These are professional hand-sewing needles. They are short, and are therefore quick and easy to use, provided they are held properly with two fingers and the side of the thimble. They encourage sewers to make stitches in one movement from start to finish, so making it easier to do rows of identical, neat, small stitches — a mark of the professional.

Bias
A bias is a line on the fabric not on the straight grain but also not on the true cross.

Bodkin
This is a bone or plastic pointed tool used for removing bastings and tackings without damaging the fabric.

Bridle
This is the stay, usually of tape or linen, that runs along a lapel roll line into the collar and partly round the back of the neck.

Buttonhole twist
Buttonhole twist is a thick thread, often silk, for hand-worked buttonholes on coats and jackets.

Canvas
Canvas is used for interfacing coats and jackets. It is generally made of flax. Various weights are available to suit different fabrics. Collar canvas is very stiff and usually made of cotton. Shrink before use by sprinkling with water and pressing.

Cross or true cross
This is a line on the fabric exactly midway between the warp and weft threads (i.e. at 45° to the straight grain of the fabric).

Curtain or skirt
The curtain is the extra piece of lining or silesia extending below the waistband of men's trousers to cover the join and prevent stretching when a commercial banding is not being used.

Domette
A soft fluffy open-weave fabric, domette is used for padding the chest area of ladies' coats and jackets.

Donkey
A donkey is a large padded sleeveboard for tailoring. It has two arms of different sizes; both arms may be padded to give four different sized ends for pressing, or the small side may be of plain wood to provide a hard surface for some of the pressing involved in tailoring with good quality worsted cloth.

Felling
Felling is rather like hemming stitch, but is stronger and deeper and less visible. It is used for attaching linings. Work from right to left inserting the needle fairly deeply into the cloth but not through to the right side. It should be virtually invisible. A good felling stitch is worked no more than 2 mm ($\frac{1}{16}$ in) apart. Leave the thread loose to avoid puckering.

Flash-basting
Flash-basting is upright basting but with a back stitch worked horizontally at each stitch. It is stronger than basting, and is used for joining linings to seam turnings.

Fly
This is a concealed opening with a flap covering the fastening, which may be a zip or buttons.

Forepart
This is the front section of a coat or jacket.

Gimp
Gimp is a thick silk-covered wiry thread used for putting in hand-worked buttonholes in coats.

Gimp needle
This is a big needle with a round eye large enough to take gimp.

Goose
A heavy tailoring iron is known as a goose. It can be heated by gas or electricity, or it can be a flat iron.

Gorge
Gorge is the visible hand-drawn seam between collar and lapel, worked from the right side.

Haircloth or laptair
This mixture of cotton and horsehair is available in various weights according to the cloth being used. In tailoring it is used for supporting the chest and front edge of coats and jackets.

Ham
A firm padded cushion, oval in shape, a ham is inserted under the bust or chest areas when pressing.

Hole-and-button cuff
This term is used to describe a tailored cuff opening fastened with one to four buttons. The buttonholes are often worked without cutting the cloth and the buttons are sewn on top. The exception is with a blazer-type button where there is a shank to conceal. In this case proper buttonholes have to be made.

Holland
Holland is linen cloth of fine texture, used in tailoring for reinforcing and for stays. Shrink before using.

Jigger
The inside button on a double-breasted coat used to hold the underneath in position is known as a jigger.

Kick-tape
This is strong tape in basic colours which is inserted on the inside edge of men's trouser hems to prevent wear.

Lambswool
Lambswool is used, when available, for sleeve-head supports. Tailor's felt can also be used.

Lapel
The lapel is the part of the jacket front that rolls back between the collar end and the top button.

Layer
To layer is to trim down a number of raw edges to

different widths to reduce bulk and lessen the chance of a ridge.

Melton

Melton is a close, durable wool, thin and firm almost like felt. It is used for tailored under-collars as it does not fray, and is available in basic dark colours and in white.

Nap

The nap is the collective name for the fine hairs of a faced cloth or the pile of velvet, all running in one direction. The term nap has come to include any cloth that is one-way.

Pressing block

A smooth wooden pressing block is required for banging steam into seams, pleats, creases and stubborn areas, after removing the iron and the damp cloth.

Prick stitch

This stitch can also be referred to as hand-picking. It consists of an invisible back stitch, made by inserting the needle behind where the thread emerges. The stitch taken underneath is as small as the fabric allows. If the fabric is thick the needle will have to be stabbed through from side to side. It is used for stitching zips, and working a swelled edge.

Punch

A punch is a tool used for punching holes to make tailored buttonholes and belt eyelets.

Roll line

The roll line is the line on which a collar or lapel rolls into its natural position round the neck.

RS

In dressmaking instructions, RS is the abbreviation for 'right side' (of the fabric).

Selvedge

The firm finished edge of a length of fabric is known as the selvedge. Threads parallel to this are often referred to as selvedge threads.

Serging

Serging is the tailoring term for overcasting a raw edge to prevent fraying. It is a deep stitch, and can also be used where a raw edge has to be actually caught down onto a layer underneath.

Silesia

Sometimes referred to as 'pocketing', silesia is a closely-woven strong cotton fabric in basic tailoring colours and white, used for making pocket bags in coats and jackets.

Sleeve lining

Strong, closely woven silk or rayon taffeta (usually cream with grey stripes) is used for lining men's jacket sleeves. It is generally more durable than the body lining.

St y

This reinforcement is made of linen tape, stay tape or strips of selvedge cut from the lining to support pockets, prevent lapels stretching, etc.

Stay tape

A narrow cotton tape with a selvedge on both sides, can be used at the edge of the canvas on the front edge of a coat from hem to gorge, or it can be used for the bridle. Shrink before use.

Step

The step is the angle between the lapel and the collar.

Stiletto

A pointed steel tool is used for forcing a hole in fabric and for re-shaping the round end of a buttonhole after stitching.

Swelled edge

This is the invisibly hand-stitched edge round the collar, lapels, pocket flaps, etc, on a tailored garment.

Tailor's soap

A hard, dry, yellow soap (available in blocks), tailor's soap is rubbed dry on the wrong side of the cloth under seam turnings, pleats and trouser creases, before pressing, to achieve a crisper finish.

Tailor's tacks

Also called mark stitches or thread marks, these are tufts of double tacking thread inserted to mark turnings, balance marks, etc.

Trouser pocketing

This is a strong fabric made in various weights in anything from cotton to nylon for use only in trousers.

Vent or hack

This is the slit in the back of a jacket. There may be a single one at the centre back, or one in each side-panel seam. Always fit the garment with the vent basted up.

Wadding

Thick fluffy cotton or synthetic fabric with a shiny papery surface is used as wadding for shoulder pads and for padding coats out to disguise figure faults. Wadding can be split to any thickness.

Waistbanding

A commercially produced strip, incorporating a rubber grip, is used to line the inside of men's trouser waistbands. It is made wide enough to cover the band and also hang below, so eliminating the necessity for a curtain.

WS

In dressmaking instructions, ws is the abbreviation for 'wrong side' (of the fabric).

Pressing equipment

Sleeve board

A good wooden sleeve board is essential. If it is not possible to buy one, a board can be constructed at home. Use a heavy wood, with a finished thickness of 2.5 cm (1 in). All edges must be rounded for ease of use. The support column should be secured by wood adhesive and two countersunk screws through the top and base (fig 1).

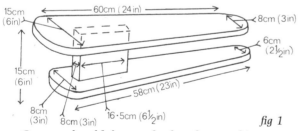

fig 1

Covers should be made for the working surfaces. The narrow end of a cover should be sewn closed, and the wide end should be left open and elasticated. The cover will thus form a sleeve into which the board can slide. Underneath thickness can be created by using pieces of old blanket, with elasticated edges, to fit around the board.

Cover the top of the bare wooden board with a single layer of blanket (not foam) cut exactly to size. This may be stuck down with adhesive. Make a fitted cotton cover to fit over the blanket. Place pieces of fabric, cut roughly to shape but with at least 5 cm (2 in) extra all round, with RS to the board, covering the whole of the top and the underneath section as far as the support column. Pin together accurately round the edges. Machine. Trim the edges. Turn in a wide hem round the remainder of the cover, and insert the elastic. The cover should fit closely to prevent accidental creases making marks on the fabric being pressed. Cover the narrow arm of the board with a fitted cotton cover only, and use this for pressing firm woollens and worsteds.

Pressing pad

There is a selection of pads available on the market of varying sizes, but a soft pad for general use can be made at home. Cut an oval of firm card about 15–20 cm (6–8 in) long. Pile a filling (e.g. cut-up tights) on the top and make a fitted cover in strong cotton, such as calico, leaving a small opening to stuff in extra filling to make it firm. Sew up the opening. Make a detachable cotton cover by cutting an oval larger than the top of the pad and putting two or three rows of shirring round the edge (fig 2).

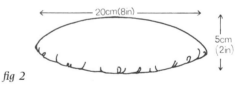

fig 2

Pressing block

A wooden pressing block is useful for pressing hems and pleats. Use a block of wood about 25 cm × 6 cm × 6 cm (10 in × 2½ in × 2½ in), ensuring that the surfaces are very smooth – the bottom surface particularly. A handle may be made by shaping a ridge along the top (fig 3).

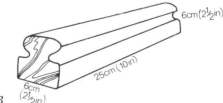

fig 3

Making up a Garment

The order of making up a garment is most important. With some dresses, blouses and skirts, the order may be influenced by certain style details, but always follow the correct order of make up as far as possible; set in sleeves fairly late to avoid crushing them while working on other sections, and deal with the hem last so that the complete garment is hanging as it will in wear. There are, of course, exceptions: a blouse hem can be made at any stage.

With a jacket, coat, trousers and man's shirt, there is a set routine which makes construction easier and this should always be followed. With these garments (as with all others) first tack up for a fitting, and then take the garment apart to begin constructing. Remember to stop and fit at every major stage.

Man's or lady's coat or jacket
1. Darts
2. Pockets
3. Interfacing
4. Front facings
5. Side and centre back seams
6. Vent
7. Hem
8. Lining
9. Shoulders
10. Collar
11. Sleeves: seams
     cuff
     lining
12. Buttonholes
13. Buttons
14. Press

Man's trousers
1. Darts and front pleats
2. Back pocket
3. Outside leg seams
4. Inside leg seams
5. Press creases
6. Side pockets
7. First side zip and fly (right)
8. Waistbands and curtain
9. Crutch seam
10. Second side zip and fly (left)
11. Fastening
12. Hems and kick-tape
13. Press

Lady's trousers
1. Darts
2. Outside leg seams
3. Inside leg seams
4. Press creases
5. Crutch seam
6. Zip
7. Waistband
8. Fastening
9. Hems
10. Press

Man's shirt
1. Yoke seams and yoke lining
2. Fold and stitch centre front bands
3. Collar
4. Insert sleeves
5. Side and sleeve seam in one
6. Hem
7. Sleeve openings and cuffs
8. Buttonholes and buttons

Darts

Darts in fine fabrics may be pressed to one side after stitching. If the fabric is bulky the fold of the dart should be cut and the dart pressed open to reduce the bulk (fig 4).

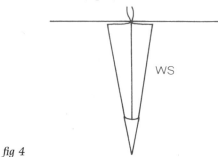

WS

fig 4

Press the dart to one side and the melton will fall into a double fold the other way (fig 6).

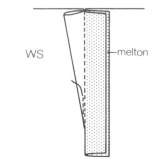

WS —melton

fig 6

If, however, you are making a small dart in thick fabric, it would be impossible to open it because of the likelihood of the narrow edge of fabric fraying away. Yet, if you leave it double and press it to one side it will form a ridge. To overcome this place a narrow piece of soft cloth, such as melton, under the dart and machine through the dart and cloth at the same time. Make sure the melton is on the opposite side to the direction in which the dart will be pressed (fig 5).

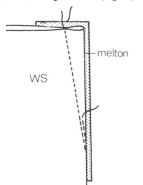

—melton

WS

fig 5

Pleats

There are three main types of pleat, knife, inverted and box; all are made by folding the fabric. Sometimes the backs of pleats are cut separately to give a better hang to the garment or in order to economise on fabric. Always begin by marking all pleat lines with tailor's tacks; also mark the hemline if possible. Good, prolonged pressing is essential.

Knife pleats

If the skirt has knife pleats all round, it is easier to establish the skirt length and turn up and finish the hem completely before inserting the pleats.

Working from the RS, fold the pleats, matching tailor's tack lines, then tack from hem to waist. Press well with a hot iron over a damp cloth. If the pleats are to be stitched down for part of the way, do this now. It helps to hold the pleats in position in wear if the back folds are machined at this stage. Begin at the hem and stitch up to the waist (fig 7).

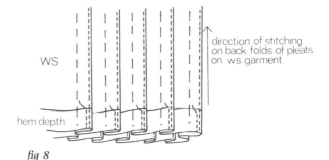

fig 8

If the skirt has only a few knife pleats it is best to set them in position from the WS. With the fabric WS up, fold over each pleat, matching up the tailor's tacks. Tack from hem to waist (fig 8). If the pleats are to be stitched down for part of their length, do this now on the WS (fig 9). Press well

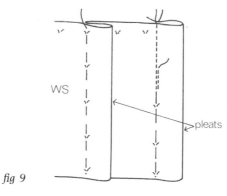

fig 9

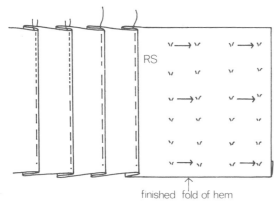

fig 7

from the RS, making sure all pleats are facing in the correct direction. Finish the skirt, then turn up the hem. To do this remove the tacks in the pleats, open out the fabric, then turn up and finish the hem (fig 10). Refold the pleats, and hold them in

15

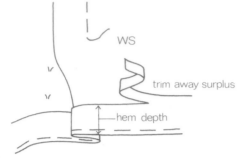

fig 10

position with a double basting stitch through the hem. Press, placing a towel against the inner edge to prevent a ridge showing (fig 11).

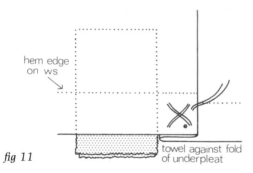

fig 11

To keep the pleats in position, stitch down the folds on the backs of the pleats and through the hem.

If the pleat is in two pieces (if there is an actual seam at the back of the pleat instead of a fold), tack the pleat in the usual way, press, and stitch the seam. Turn up the hem with the seam trimmed and pressed open within the hem. Snip the seam turnings at the top of the hem, then neaten the turnings above the hem. Stitch the fold of the pleat through the hem (fig 12).

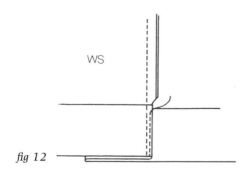

fig 12

Inverted pleats

These will remain in position best if the pleat backing is cut separately. If the pattern is in one piece, you can cut off the part that forms the pleat backing, and cut it out in fabric separately.

Place the fabric RS together, matching tailor's tacks, and tack. Mark with chalk the depth the pleat is to be stitched. Machine from the chalk mark up to the waist. Alter the machine stitch to the largest available, and machine from the chalk line down to the hem. Remove all tacks and press open (fig 13). This is virtually the final pressing of

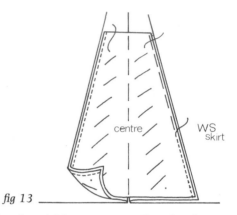

fig 13

the pleat folds, so press well with a hot iron, damp cloth and plenty of pressure. Use a pressing block to bang in the steam after removing the cloth. Leave each section until cold before pressing the next section.

Place the pleat backing in position on the ws, RS down. Baste the backing to the pleat edges. Draw a chalk line down the raw edge on each side. Tack on the line through the two layers and machine (fig 14).

fig 14

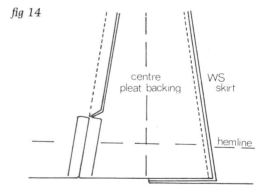

After completing the rest of the skirt, remove the large machine stitches and turn up the hem. Make sure the seam is trimmed and pressed open where it falls inside the hem. Snip the turnings of the seam at the top of the hem. Neaten the raw edges. Stitch through the pleat fold after basting the pleats in position (fig 15).

fig 15

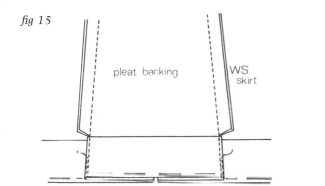

pleat backing   WS skirt

Box pleats

A box pleat is two knife pleats put together. Fold the fabric, matching the tailor's tacks, and stitch from the ws from the required depth to the hem (fig 16). Machine to the hem using a large stitch.

fig 16

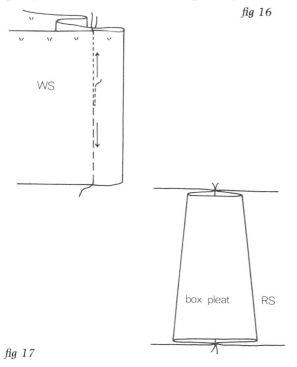

WS

Press well, opening the fabric before pressing to one side (fig 17). The box pleat can then be sewn down at the sides (fig 18).

fig 18

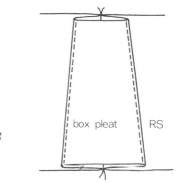

box pleat   RS

box pleat   RS

fig 17

1   *Skirt showing inverted and box pleats*

Pockets

Pockets are one of the most difficult processes to work successfully, because they must look neat and yet be strong enough to withstand constant use. Also, most types of pocket are conspicuous, often forming part of the style of the garment.

Tailors always hope that pockets are not going to be used, because they tend to pull the garment out of shape when they are filled with bulky objects. With the exception of men's trouser pockets and inside jacket pockets, it is much better if they are used as little as possible, and then only perhaps to hold a bus ticket. A good tailor will always measure a man's wallet and allow for its thickness so that it will not distort the coat. This service is especially important if the wearer is a professional man, such as a doctor who must always carry a prescription pad. My father never carried anything in any of his jacket pockets; he kept his money in a very small note case in his trouser pocket.

Types of pockets
There are three main types of pockets: patch pockets, cut pockets, and seam pockets.

Patch pockets are used on sporting jackets for men's and ladies' coats and jackets; they involve attaching a piece of the same or contrasting material to the outside of the garment.

With cut pockets, a cut is made in the garment fabric, and the pocket material is sewn inside the garment. Jetted pockets are those with a narrow piping on each side; they can also have flaps. They are used on the body of a jacket, as an inside breast pocket, as a back trouser pocket (sometimes buttoned), and as a ticket pocket (which is a small pocket within one of the main pockets on a coat).

A welt pocket uses a wider strip of fabric, and can be designed slightly sloping and curved, as with a man's breast pocket, or the main pockets on a lady's coat.

A flap pocket, which can be used on coats and jackets, can be straight or sloping with the ends parallel with the front edge of the coat; the corners are slightly rounded. The lower edge is finished with a narrow jetting. A jetted flap pocket has a narrow jetting along the top of the flap where it joins the coat.

Seam pockets are used in ladies' coats, skirts, dresses and trousers, and are often made by simply folding back the seam turning and adding a pocket bag. Seam pockets in men's trousers have to withstand a lot of wear, so they are made by adding extra fabric to the seam edges.

Rules for all pockets
Always reinforce the ws of the garment where the pocket is to be made. The strip of reinforcement should be 4 cm (1½ in) longer than the pocket and 4 cm (1½ in) wide. It can be of linen, soft canvas, or iron-on or sew-in *Vilene*. If two matching pockets are to be placed on each side of the body, place the two garment sections together and tailor tack the position, marking across the ends with tailor's tacks. Open out the pieces, but mark the pocket line with chalk on top of the tailor's tacks before starting the pocket.

When machining pockets, make a chalk line on which to stitch to ensure accuracy of position as well as length.

Support cut pockets further, when finished, by back stitching a narrow piece of linen or a length of stay tape to the top corner of the pocket nearest the side seam, and back stitch the other end to the seam turnings or armhole turnings.

Work strong bar tacks at each end of the pocket when finished. On welts and jettings these are normal bar tacks; on welt pockets the prick stitching across the end is sufficient; on patch pockets work a tiny french tack under the corner to take the strain.

The grain of the welt, patch, flap or jetting must be on the same grain as the jacket, or it can be directly on the cross for effect. If it is on the straight, any pattern must match exactly. Do this by marking the pocket position with chalk, lay a spare piece of cloth on top matching the pattern, and chalk the exact size and shape of the piece needed and cut out, adding turnings. All jacket pockets should have an additional support of a linen strip $2\frac{1}{2}$ cm (1 in) wide from the outer corner of the pocket running up to the armhole seam (see fig 43, page 26), and similarly from the breast pocket outer edge to the armhole seam.

On trouser pockets always work a double row of stitching round the bag for strength.

Pocket bags should be slightly wider at the bottom front edge, and should have rounded corners to prevent catching fluff and small coins.

After making a pocket, always close it up with basting and press, then leave the stitches in until the garment is finished.

Sizes of pockets

The width of the pocket can be calculated by measuring the hand across and adding a little ease, if the hand is to go into the pocket. The size of the bag can be calculated in the same way, just big enough to take the hand. When the hand is in the pocket the top must not be wrinkled up. On a jacket the size of the bag may be governed by the length of the jacket. Patch pockets can be larger purely for effect. The following sizes are a guide:

Breast pocket: welt 11×2.5 cm ($4\frac{1}{4} \times 1$ in); bag, 14×13 cm ($5\frac{1}{2} \times 5$ in).
Body pocket: (man's) width 17 cm ($6\frac{3}{4}$ in); bag, 20×18 cm ($8 \times 7\frac{1}{4}$ in) (lady's) 12 cm ($4\frac{3}{4}$ in); bag, 15×14 cm ($6 \times 5\frac{1}{2}$ in).
Patch pocket: (man's) width 18 cm ($7\frac{1}{4}$ in); depth, 20 cm (8 in); (lady's) 13 cm (5 in); depth,   17 cm   ($6\frac{3}{4}$ in).

Welts are made according to taste on body pockets but are about 3–4 cm (1–$1\frac{1}{2}$ in) in depth on a coat.

Flaps are made to taste but are usually about 4 to 7 cm ($1\frac{1}{2}$ to $2\frac{3}{4}$ in) deep.

Jettings are made as narrow and as neat as the thickness of the cloth will allow.

Bags are easier to make if rectangles of fabric are cut roughly to the correct size, but delay marking the exact size or shape of the bag until both bag pieces are attached and are ready to be joined together. This is particularly helpful when adding a pocket bag to a pocket which has already been started, but even with simple pockets it is often best not to decide on the exact size of the bag until after the pocket has been made.

Patch pockets

If the fabric is soft or floppy, interface the ws with a suitable weight of sew-in or iron-on interfacing.

Unlined pockets

Turn in the top edge of the pocket and tack along the fold; press. Hold down the raw edge with a fabric adhesive (such as *Wundaweb*), with herringbone stitch or with a row of machining. Turn in the other three edges on the fitting line and tack. If the corners are rounded they should be snipped. Press. Place in position and tack round all four sides to hold (fig 19).

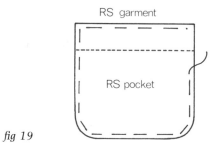

fig 19

Work a very small slip stitch, just under the edge, round three sides (fig 20). (For the purpose of clarity, the stitching in the illustration is shown very loosely stitched.) Work bar tacks at the top corners just inside the corners.

Lined pockets

Turn in all outside edges as above and hold down with fabric adhesive or herringbone stitch.

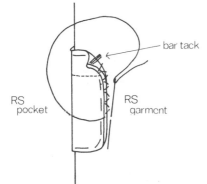

fig 20

Cut pieces of lining fabric the same size plus turnings. Place to the pocket ws together, and baste. Trim the raw edges and turn under all round. Along the top edge the lining should just cover the raw edges, the lining is therefore about 1–2 cm ($\frac{3}{8}$–$\frac{3}{4}$ in) below the top edge of the pocket. Round the other three sides, the edge of the lining should be about 2 mm ($\frac{1}{16}$ in) back from the edge (fig 21). Tack. Fell all round. Remove tacks, and press.

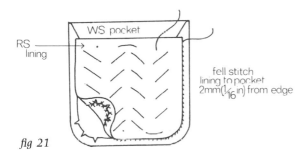

fell stitch lining to pocket 2mm($\frac{1}{16}$in) from edge

fig 21

If top stitching is required do it at this stage either by machine or by hand (see swelled edge, page 103).

If a box or inverted pleat is put in a patch pocket, insert the pleat and stitch it, then line the pocket as described.

Place the pockets in position, and attach by hand. If the edge has been stitched it looks better to work the slip stitch further in (ie under the edge-stitching).

Flap pockets

Making the flaps without interfacing

Place lining and cloth pieces RS together with the cloth piece uppermost. Tack round, easing the cloth slightly on the lining to prevent the lining from showing along the edge and the flap curling up. Machine round. Trim, snip, and turn through, then roll the edges so that the lining is slightly to the underside. Baste the edge, and press. Finally work the swelled edge (page 103) if desired.

Making the flaps with interfacing

Interfacing is not normally needed in suitings but it may be a good idea in some loose or soft fabrics. Cut the interfacing pieces exactly to flap size, without turnings. Press or baste in place. If using sew-in interfacing, attach it by herringboning all round. Turn in the edges of the flap over the interfacing round three sides, not across the top. Snip well at the corners. Tack, press, and trim, then herringbone down (fig 22).

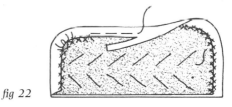

fig 22

Place the lining pieces with ws down to the ws flap, turn the edges in, tack, and fell down with the edge of the lining a little back from the edge of the flap (fig 23). Press. Work the swelled edge (page 103) if desired.

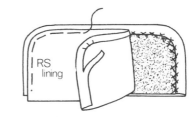

fig 23

Baste the lining to the flap along the raw edges, pulling the lining up slightly to help the flap to curl under.

Place the flap with RS down to the RS of the coat, with the seam line exactly over the chalk line marking the pocket position. Baste. Make a chalk line on the flap on which to machine, as it is difficult to be accurate once the work is under the machine. Machine exactly from end to end of the flap (fig 24).

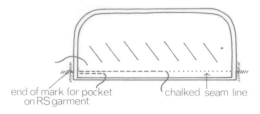

end of mark for pocket
on RS garment

chalked seam line

fig 24

Cut a piece of cloth 5 cm (2 in) deep, and wider than the pocket, and join it to a piece of pocketing. Place this RS down below the pocket line. Baste. Machine 3 mm ($\frac{1}{8}$ in) from the previous row of stitching, making this line slightly shorter than the top row at each end (fig 25).

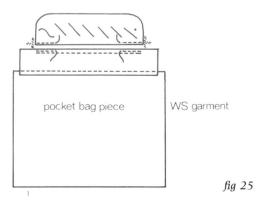

pocket bag piece   WS garment

fig 25

Cut the pocket by snipping between the rows of stitching. Work from the ws and cut through the fabric and reinforcement only. Cut right to the ends of the machining.

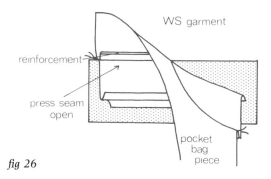

WS garment

reinforcement

press seam open

pocket bag piece

fig 26

Pass the lower piece through to the ws, trim the turnings, and press open the join (fig 26). Form a jetting by rolling the edge until it is very narrow, then prick stitch along the join (fig 27).

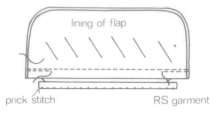

lining of flap

prick stitch   RS garment

fig 27

Bring the flap down and press the join from the RS, then baste the flap down.

Cut a piece of pocketing and place it against the flap turnings on the ws. Machine as close as possible to the row of stitching holding the flap in position.

Work a row of prick stitches from the RS through the turnings just above the flap join (fig 28).

Push under the triangles at each end. Mark the size and shape of the pocket bag and machine, stitching as close as possible to the ends of the pocket, catching in the triangles if possible.

Work a bar tack across the ends of the pocket beside the flap to the lower edge of the jetting, then press (fig 28).

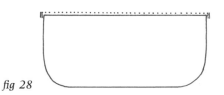

fig 28

Jetted pockets

These are sometimes called piped pockets (fig 29). Cut three pieces of cloth (one for backing the opening) 6 cm (2$\frac{1}{2}$ in) deep and 2 cm ($\frac{3}{4}$ in) longer than the pocket size. Join one piece to a

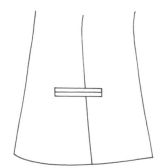

fig 29

2   *Dress showing jetted pockets*

piece of pocketing, then press the join with the turnings towards the pocketing.

Place this piece RS down against the pocket line on the RS of the coat, below the line, and the other piece RS down above. The raw edges must be close together. Machine 3 mm ($\frac{1}{8}$ in) from each raw edge. The rows of stitching must be parallel and the same length (fig 30).

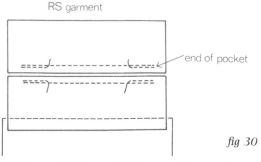

fig 30

Cut the pocket by snipping on the WS through the reinforcement and the garment only. Cut between the rows and then out to the corners, snipping right up to the end of the machining. Press open all seams (fig 31), then pass the strips through the slit to the WS (fig 32).

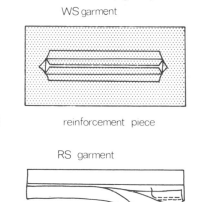

fig 31   reinforcement piece

fig 32

If the pocket is to be used frequently, the lower edge will strain in wear, so reinforce it by slipping a length of stay tape under the lower jetting. Back stitch it to the reinforcing fabric close to the machining.

Pass both pieces to the WS.

Roll and tack the jettings to form a narrow piping of even width along both edges. Prick stitch through the join from the RS, then press (fig 33).

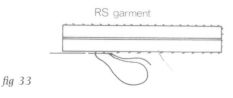

fig 33

Join the third strip of fabric 6 cm (2$\frac{1}{2}$ in) deep to a piece of pocketing to form the other side of the bag.

fig 34

If there is to be an inside ticket pocket make it now from two pieces of pocketing. This pocket should be about 9 cm (3$\frac{1}{2}$ in) wide and 5 cm (2 in) below the top edge.

On the WS of the coat, place this pocket bag piece RS down onto the back of the pocket with the raw edge level with the raw edge of the top jetting. Hold the bag edge and jetting edge together and baste. Machine as close as possible to the top of the pocket or it will hang down. It is worth using the zip foot for this (fig 34).

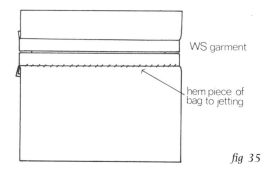

fig 35

On the RS push the triangles of cloth (which have formed) underneath the end of the pocket. Do this with the point of a needle.

Place both bag pieces together, chalk the shape of the pocket bag on the top one and machine round (fig 36). Begin and end very close to the pocket mouth and catch in the little triangles if you can. Work two rows and trim (fig 37).

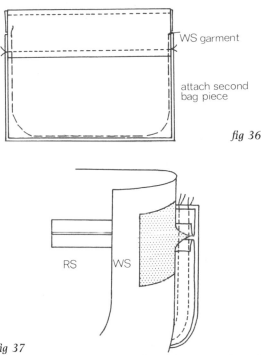

fig 36

attach second
bag piece

WS garment

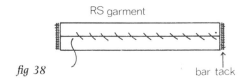

RS   WS

fig 37

On the RS baste the pocket edges together (fig 38). Work a bar tack through all the layers across the width of the jettings, then press.

RS garment

fig 38   bar tack

Inside breast pocket

This is a jetted pocket made using pieces of lining to make the jettings (fig 39). It can have a zip.

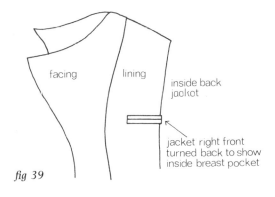

facing   lining

inside back
jacket

jacket right front
turned back to show
inside breast pocket

fig 39

Trouser back pocket

This can be a jetted pocket or a very narrow welt, sometimes fastened for safety with a button (fig 40). If jetted it must have a fabric facing across the trouser opening as for the coat jetted pocket.

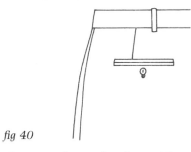

fig 40

Support the pocket by cutting the bag pieces long enough to extend up to the waistband so that it can be stitched inside the waistband later. This can be one long piece of pocketing with a piece of cloth stitched to it which falls at the back of the pocket opening.

Flap and jetted pockets

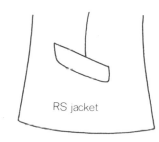

RS jacket

fig 41

Attach the jettings as described for a jetted pocket. Turn them through and prick stitch in the joins.

Push the triangles underneath at each end. Make up the flap 2 mm ($\frac{1}{16}$ in) longer than the pocket. Push the flap into the slit and baste, making sure that the flap looks evenly placed (fig 42). Turn to the ws and machine through the

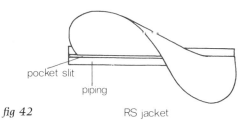

pocket slit

piping

fig 42   RS jacket

flap and jetting as close as possible to the prick stitching in the jetting.

Finish as for a flap or jetted pocket. ·

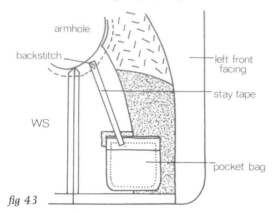

fig 43

Welt pocket

Cut a piece of fabric on the straight grain with the pattern matching the area of the garment. Use fabric on the bias only for a decorative effect.

Attach the interfacing cut to exactly the size required for the finished welt. Attach to the ws of the welt piece (fig 44).

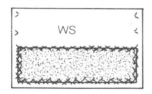

fig 44

Turn in the ends of the welt over the interfacing, then baste, press, trim down, and herringbone (fig 45).

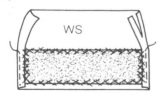

fig 45

Trim the edges of the other half of the welt at a slight angle, so that, when turned in and folded down, the edges are slightly to the underside of the welt. Baste the top and ends. Press and slip stitch (fig 46).

Place the welt on the RS of the garment, ws up. The position of the welt is below the marked pocket line, so that when the welt is folded up into position the open edge is correctly placed. Baste

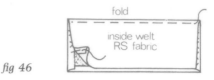

fig 46

and machine the welt, taking a normal turning. Stitch exactly from end to end but do not allow the stitching to extend over the ends of the welt. Trim down the raw edge of the welt (fig 47).

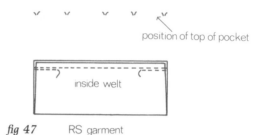

fig 47   RS garment

Place a piece of pocket bag RS down above the welt with its raw edge against the raw edges of the welt. Baste and machine, taking only a 3 mm ($\frac{1}{8}$ in) turning. This row of stitching must be shorter at each end than the row below (fig 48).

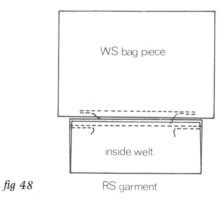

fig 48   RS garment

On the ws of the garment cut between the rows of stitching and out to the ends of the stitching (fig 49).

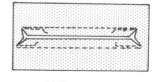

fig 49   WS garment

3   *Sleeveless dress showing welt pockets*

Push the pocket bag through the slit and allow it to hang down inside the garment. Press the join open. Push the fabric triangles to the ws. Fold the welt up to cover the opening. Press the join with the toe of the iron. Baste the welt down firmly. Slip stitch the ends strongly, and work a row of prick stitch parallel with the ends, but stab stitching through all the layers of fabric (fig 50).

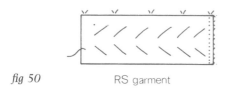

fig 50 RS garment

On the ws press over a narrow turning on the other piece of pocket bag; place this fold on the machine stitches attaching the welt, then baste and hem (fig 51).

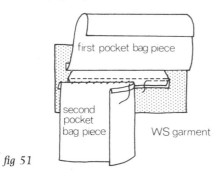

first pocket bag piece

second pocket bag piece   WS garment

fig 51

Bring the first piece of pocket bag down. Baste the two pieces together round the outer edge. Chalk the correct size and shape of bag for the garment, with rounded corners. Machine round the bag, starting very close to the ends of the pocket. Work two parallel rows of machining and overcast the edge if necessary (fig 52).

WS bag piece

fig 52   WS garment

Seam pockets

These are usually found only in women's clothes. Reinforce the fitting line with a strip of interfacing. Fold back the turning at the front of the garment and press. Stitch with machining, or prick stitch if you want the pocket opening to show.

Cut a rectangle of fabric 4 cm (1½ in) wide and the depth of the pocket. Attach it to the turnings at the back of the garment. Cut two pocket bag pieces (usually lining); stitch one piece to the rectangle of fabric and the other to the turning at the front of the garment. Press. Mark the shape of the bag and machine round.

In light-weight fabrics the whole bag may be cut in garment fabric, cutting the bag all in one with the garment.

Men's side-seam trouser pockets

Baste a strip of linen 6 cm (2½ in) wide and 26 cm (10½ in) long against the edge of the front trouser leg.

Cut two pieces of cloth 5 cm (2 in) wide and 23 cm (9¼ in) long. Place one on the front leg and one on the back, RS together. The top of the pocket opening comes 5 cm (2 in) down from the waist, so that is the position for the pieces. Stitch in position (fig 53).

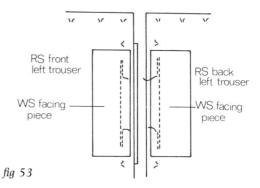

RS front left trouser

WS facing piece

RS back left trouser

WS facing piece

fig 53

Sew the back and front trouser legs together at the side seam, sewing down from the waist for a distance of 5 cm (2 in). Press open.

On the front trouser, roll the facing strip back to the ws. Baste, press and prick stitch 5 mm (³⁄₁₆ in) in from the edge.

On the outer edge of the back piece turn a

narrow hem, and machine or prick stitch to hold flat.

Make a pocket bag from a piece of trouser pocketing 40 cm (16 in) wide and deep enough to include not only the pocket opening and the depth of the hand but also sufficient height for it to extend up into the waistband later.

Trim the bag slightly so that it measures about 18 cm (7 in) across the top (doubled).

Place in position against the facings and attach the front side first. Fold the top layer of the bag back and baste 4 cm ($1\frac{1}{2}$ in) in from the raw edge. Turn in the raw edge of the pocket and baste so that the edge is 2 cm ($\frac{3}{4}$ in) back from the trouser edge. Fell this edge very firmly. Join the two lower edges of the bag with a curved french seam (fig 54).

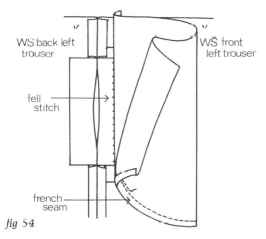

WS back left trouser

WS front left trouser

fell stitch

french seam

fig 54

From the RS baste up the pocket opening.

Back stitch the pocket to the extension piece. Work from the pocket side, feeling the position of the edge of the extension underneath.

Turn in the raw edge of the pocket where it falls on the trouser seam and fell it to the seam turnings.

At the base of the pocket strongly hem the pocket where it crosses the side seam of the trouser. On the RS work a strong bar tack at the top and bottom of the pocket, across the seam.

Interfacing

Nearly all garments need reinforcing at some point. A layer of interfacing of a suitable type and weight for the fabric should be placed against the ws of the garment in all areas of strain or constant use, where a tricky process is to be worked, or where crispness in appearance is required. Interfacing correctly chosen and inserted improves the appearance and the wearing qualities of a garment.

Whether or not the pattern being used suggests it, consider where interfacing might be used to advantage. In addition to the obvious places like collars, cuffs, waistbands and overlapping openings, interfacing improves yokes, patch pockets, pocket flaps and welts, tie belts, small contrasting inserts, midriff areas, and sleeve bands. It can also be used to stabilize such fabrics as knits and before a process is worked, such as inserting a zip.

There is an interfacing suitable for every type of fabric. Some have to be sewn in position; some can be ironed in place. Thin sew-in varieties can be cut to the full size of the area and caught in with the seams later. Heavier types should be cut without turnings, basted carefully to the ws of the fabric, and caught down with catch stitch or herringbone stitch all round.

With iron-on varieties, cut to the full size of the area, but trim off 3 mm ($\frac{1}{8}$ in) all round before pressing in place, to prevent the edge sticking to the ironing surface. The edges will be caught in with the seams.

Where a free edge of interfacing falls as it would down beside an opening, on heavy fabrics lightly catch stitch it to the fabric. On others, slip a few short lengths of fabric adhesive (such as *Wundaweb*) between the interfacing and the fabric, and press.

Types of interfacing

1. For light and sheer fabrics, from chiffon and voile to polyester/cotton and lawn, use light sew-in or transparent iron-on interfacing, or a layer of self-fabric or cotton lawn.
2. For medium-weight fabrics, from linen-weave polyester and sailcloth to denim and firm cotton, use soft, light, or medium sew-in, or soft or firm iron-on interfacing.
3. For light-weight jersey or knitted fabrics, choose a light or soft sew-in or transparent iron-on interfacing.
4. For firm jersey, and light woven woollens and acrylics, an iron-on interfacing which stretches (such as *Superdrape*) is best.
5. For heavy-woven fabrics, such as brocade, the interfacing should be a medium or soft sew-in or soft iron-on.
6. For pile fabrics, use a light or soft sew-in.
7. For suiting and coating, use a medium or heavy sew-in, or firm or heavy iron-on interfacing.

Interfacing a coat or jacket

A normal suiting or coating will need canvas in the major part of the front, or forepart, with additional padding of tailor's felt or domette and haircloth (or *Laptair*) in the chest area. If a woman's coat is being made from a very soft fabric, the front can be interfaced with one layer of interfacing (such as *Vilene*), and the padding omitted. Place a rectangle of linen to be included in the front edge seam where the buttons and buttonholes will come.

Cutting

Cut the canvas to include the neck, armhole and front edge, but only two thirds of the hemline. Place the straight grain of the pattern to match the grain of the canvas. On a man's coat cut the edge curved from armhole to hem, but on a woman's coat curve it to avoid the point of an underarm bust dart.

Cut a chest piece from haircloth (or *Laptair*) on the cross to include two thirds of the armhole and shoulder, but cut it on the roll line of the lapel. Do not take it quite so far round the armhole, and curve it from there to the centre front. The haircloth is fairly stiff, so trim it back a little from the lapel roll line.

Cut the domette or tailor's felt the same shape as the haircloth. When cutting canvases etc for a man's jacket, it is as well to cut extra at the shoulder and armhole edge, and trim away after fitting.

Assembling

Stitch any darts or shaping into the canvas by overlapping. Cut darts right out, slashing to the edge of the canvas (fig 55).

Place a piece of linen tape behind, and draw the raw edges together, or simply join by zigzag stitch or herringbone (fig 56).

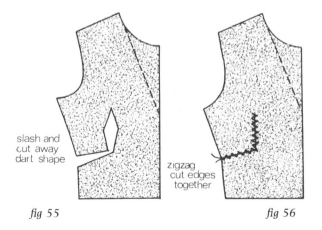

slash and cut away dart shape

zigzag cut edges together

fig 55   *fig 56*

Place the haircloth on the canvas, and the domette on top of that (fig 57). Make sure the linen tape at the back of the darts is uppermost so that it will not be placed against the cloth of the coat causing a ridge. Baste all three together.

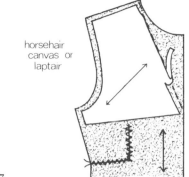

horsehair canvas or laptair

fig 57

Baste all over the chest area using tacking thread, with stitches 2.5 cm (1 in) long and the rows fairly close. The stitches must go through all layers. Do not pull the thread tight or it will cause wrinkles (fig 58).

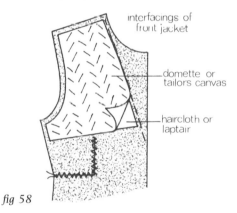

interfacings of front jacket

domette or tailors canvas

haircloth or laptair

fig 58

Press on both sides with a hot iron and a damp cloth, shaping the chest area into a curve.

Inserting

If there is a side panel join it to the coat forepart and press the seam. Place the coat front ws down onto the canvas, which should be domette side down, and baste. Work one row from just below the shoulder down to the hem, another further towards the front edge, one on the lapel roll line and another round the armhole then curving across to the dart (fig 59). As you baste, smooth out the cloth so that it is rather taut on the canvas.

As you come to a pocket, stop and back stitch the pocket turnings to the canvas for 7 cm (2¾ in) or so. Where there are front pockets, cut the canvas just below the pocket, and slip the canvas

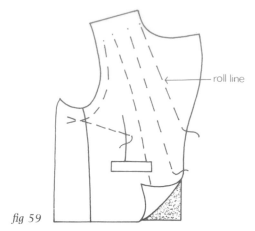

fig 59

under the pocket bag so that the canvas is up against the jacket front. Anchor the edge of the canvas by back stitching to the turning where the pocket bag joins the cloth backing (fig 60).

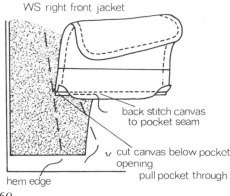

fig 60

Leave approximately 7 cm (2¾ in) clear of basting round the armhole and shoulder for easier handling at a later stage.

If working on a light-weight suiting, baste the linen to the ws of lapels as far as the roll line and up to and including the gorge. This gives more body to pad into, and there will be less chance of any actual stitches showing on the underneath of the lapel.

Padding lapels

Cut a length of tape as a bridle at least 10 cm (4 in) longer than needed. The end is later stitched round the roll of the collar. Attach the bridle; hold it firmly, and baste, then hem down each side (fig 61).

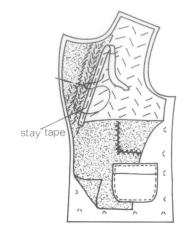

fig 61

Fold the lapel on the roll line and work pad stitch in the lapel, moving from the bridle to the outer edge of the lapel. If you hold it properly, the lapel will automatically curl correctly. (fig. 62).

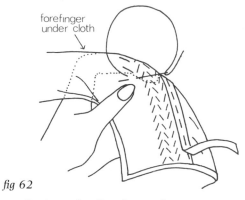

fig 62

Interfacing the back neck

If a woman's coat or jacket is made from soft loosely woven cloth, it is advisable to support the back shoulder area with soft interfacing. Use the back jacket pattern, and cut the interfacing to include the neck, armhole and shoulder down to about 5 cm (2 in) below the armhole (fig 63).

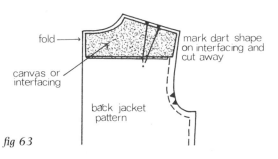

fig 63

Cut out any neck or shoulder dart, and rejoin the edges with herringbone or zigzag stitch (fig 64).

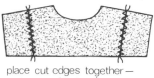

fig 64   place cut edges together — zigzag edge to edge

Place the interfacing in position on the ws of the jacket back. Baste all round the neck, shoulders and armhole 3 cm (1¼ in) in from the edge (fig 65).

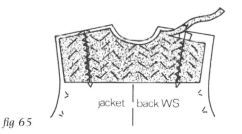

jacket back WS

fig 65

Trim the interfacing down to the fitting line along the neck and shoulders, and catch stitch over the edge (fig 66).

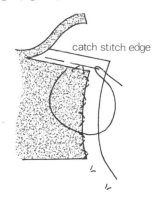

catch stitch edge

fig 66

Combined facings

These are used on sleeveless plain-necked garments. A combined facing is cut for the neck and armhole instead of having two separate facings meeting on the shoulder. The usual method of attaching the facings first and then trying to join the shoulder seams afterwards simply does not produce a good result. The following method is easier to perform, and produces a perfect finish.

Cut the interfacing from the combined facing pattern, and baste or press it to the wrong side of the garment. Join the shoulder seams, then insert the zip.

Place the front facing to the neckline, RS together; tack round the neck from shoulder to shoulder. Place the back neck facings in position and tack (fig 67).

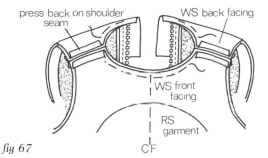

press back on shoulder seam   WS back facing   WS front facing   RS garment

fig 67   CF

Make shoulder joins in the facing by pressing the turnings back so that the creases meet, then lift the two edges and join the creases. Press open, and trim the raw edges (fig 68).

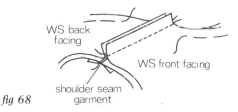

WS back facing   WS front facing   shoulder seam garment

fig 68

Machine round the neck on the fitting line. Trim, snip and roll the facing to the ws, then tack the edge and press.

Smooth the facing out on the dress on the ws, and baste all round the neck and armholes. Do not bring the basting too near the armhole edges (fig 69).

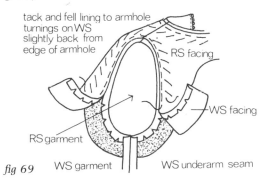

tack and fell lining to armhole turnings on WS slightly back from edge of armhole   RS facing   WS facing   RS garment   WS garment   WS underarm seam

fig 69

Working from the RS, turn in the armhole edges and tack, snipping as you tack to enable the turnings to lie flat. Trim the edge down a little, then press.

Trim a little off the raw edge of the facing. Turn in the edge of the facing, snipping where necessary, so that the edge is 2 mm ($\frac{1}{16}$ in) back from the armhole edge. At the underarm, let the front part lie flat, and turn under the back section and tack; then press (fig 70).

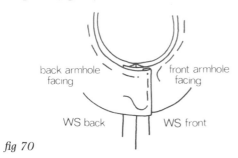

back armhole facing   front armhole facing

WS back   WS front

fig 70

Finish by felling all round, taking the needle through the turnings and interfacing only, not through to the garment layer. Neaten the outer edge of the facing. Hold this loose edge of facing down by hemming where it crosses the side seam, or place small pieces of fabric adhesive (such as *Wundaweb*) at intervals all round between the facing and the garment; then press.

Seams

Angled seam

An angled seam may be used as a style feature, or for figure emphasis. Shaping for some part of the body is often included in the seam.

Mark all fitting lines, and place one tailor's tack at the corner of the angle (fig 71).

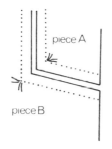

fig 71

Reinforce the angle with a small piece of soft iron-on interfacing to prevent fraying. Place the two pieces of fabric RS together matching the tailor's tacks, especially at the corner. Tack. Machine, starting with the needle precisely at the angle, work forwards a few stitches then reverse to fasten the threads, sew forwards again to the outer edge of the fabric (fig 72).

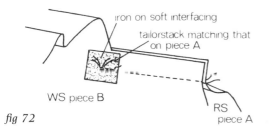

fig 72

Remove tacks. Press open as for an open seam and neaten edges. Snip into the corner exactly to the end of the stitching. Swing the top piece of fabric round until the other two raw edges meet. Match up the tailor's tacks and tack. Machine, once more starting at the corner, to avoid a pucker. Lower the needle exactly into the first stitch of the previous row, lower the foot, and machine (fig 73).

Remove tacks, press open, and neaten.

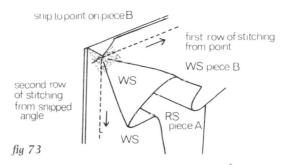

fig 73

Corded seam

Piping containing cord may be inserted in any straight or slightly shaped decorative seam, either to introduce a contrasting colour or to break the surface of a plain fabric.

This produces an attractive raised effect. Cut, join and stretch crossway strips 2.5 cm (1 in) wide; place pre-shrunk piping cord on the WS. Wrap the bias strip round the cord until the two raw edges are together. Tack beside the cord (fig 74).

fig 74

4   Evening dress with angled seam

Insert in the seam as described for the piped seam (this page), but use the piping or zip foot on the machine. Although the tacking must be accurate, it is essential to see that the edge of the foot is close up against the piping cord (fig 75).

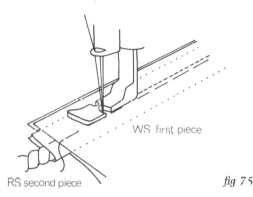

RS second piece   *fig 75*

Remove the tacks, and press carefully up to the cording but not over it. Layer the raw edges before neatening.

Machine fell seam

This is a strong flat seam used on shirts, sports wear, denim clothes, casual trousers etc. Either side can be the RS, although on fabrics such as denim the side showing the double machining looks best.

Place two pieces of fabric together, tack and machine on the fitting line. Remove tacks, and press both turnings to one side (towards the back of the garment). Turn the work over and press again to smooth out pleats or creases. Turn back to the first side and trim down the underneath turning quite narrow. The actual width will depend on the thickness of the fabric (fig 76).

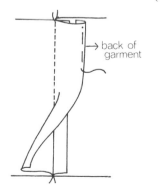

fig 76

Turn under the wider turning and tack down, creasing the fold flat first with the fingers to keep it straight. Press well. Machine along the tacked fold making sure you are using the same size stitch as for the first row of stitching if this is to be the RS of the garment (fig 77).

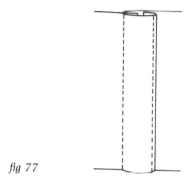

fig 77

Piped seam

A decorative seam for panels, yokes etc, the piped seam often uses a fabric that contrasts with the garment either in design or in weight and texture.

Cut strips of fabric 2.5 cm (1 in) wide on the bias. Join them if necessary, and fold in half with the WS inside, and press lightly, stretching the strip. Place the piping on the RS of one garment edge, with the fold of the piping extending a little beyond the fitting line. Tack in place exactly on the fitting line. The amount the piping extends beyond the fitting line will vary according to the fabric being used, so it is worth working a trial seam first (fig 78).

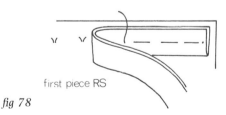

first piece RS

fig 78

Place the second piece of garment WS up on top of the piping, the raw edges all lying in one direction. Turn the work over, and tack through all layers, but tacking exactly on the previous tacking (that is, on the fitting line). Machine on this tacking (fig 79).

5   *Dress with straight seams which can be
    decorative — piped or slot seams*

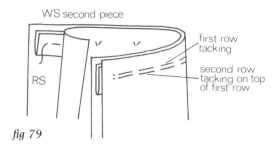

fig 79

Remove the tacks, and grade the raw edges to reduce bulk before neatening (fig 80).

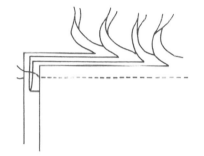

fig 80

Press on the RS by running the toe of the iron along on the edge of the fabric beside the piping. Cover the toe of the iron with a cloth to protect the fabric (fig 81).

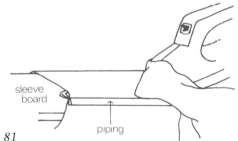

fig 81

If setting piping into a curved seam, snip the raw edges of the piping as you tack to ease it round the curves.

A special braiding can be bought which is in fact a piping attached to a narrow braid. Set the braid between the layers of fabric.

Coat shoulder seam

Fold the lining and interfacing out of the way, then tack and stitch the shoulder seams, matching up the fitting lines, and easing the fulness to the middle of the seam. Stitch and press open.

Lay the interfacing over the shoulder turnings and back stitch through all layers across the shoulder turnings (fig 82).

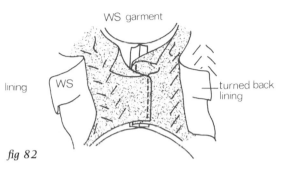

fig 82

Place the shoulder pad in position, and where it rests on the interfacing baste well to attach it. Oversew the long edge of the shoulder pad to the turnings of the armhole.

Slot seam

This is a decorative seam which can be used on any straight seams. (For curved seams, see below.) Turn in both edges of fabric on the fitting line, tack and press (fig 83).

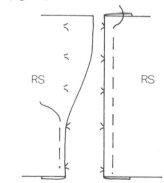

fig 83

Cut a backing strip 4 cm (1½ in) wide. This can be of self fabric or a contrast; cut on the straight or on the cross. Mark the centre of the strip with chalk or tacking (fig 84).

Place the two folded edges to the chalk line and tack. Catch the folds together with a big herring-bone stitch in tacking thread (fig 85).

Machine both folds with normal thread or top-stitching thread. Either work edge stitching close to the fold or, using the edge of the foot as a guide,

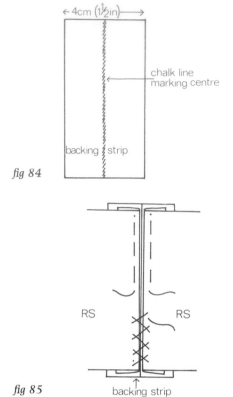

fig 84

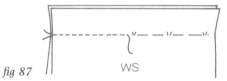

fig 85   backing strip

stitch a little further away for a tucked effect (fig 86).

Remove all tackings, and press with a damp cloth over a towel to avoid a ridge. On the WS, trim the backing and turnings down, and neaten with zigzag or overcasting. If the fabric is bulky, trim to varying widths before neatening.

To make a curved slot seam, cut shaped facings exactly the shape of the curved edges and on the same grain. Attach, trim and turn to the WS exactly as for a normal facing. Tack facings back to the WS and press. Make the seam as described above, but cutting curved backing strips.

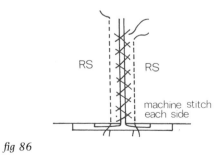

fig 86

Welt seam

A welt seam is a slightly raised seam that looks good on the sides of men's trousers and on overcoats and yoke seams. Place the two layers of fabric RS together, and machine on the fitting line (fig 87).

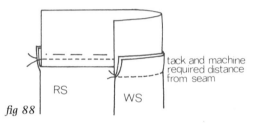

fig 87

Remove tacks and press open, then press both turnings to one side (towards the back or upwards). Work a row of stitching from the RS parallel with the seam line (fig 88).

fig 88

On light, smooth fabrics, this can be done by machine, using normal thread or top-stitching thread, but on soft fabrics or coatings of any sort the finish of the whole garment will be vastly improved by doing this stitching by hand. Use a small prick stitch, making sure that the needle goes back into the fabric only fractionally behind where it emerged, so that no thread shows at all on the RS (fig 89). Press the row of stitching with the toe of the iron.

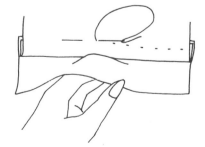

fig 89

Reinforced trouser seams

Begin by reinforcing the front fork area. Cut two squares of silesia or linen 10 cm (4 in) square; fold them in half into a triangle, and place one on the ws of each front leg. Baste them into position. Trim off the surplus at the seam edges. These will be caught in with the seam stitching later (fig 90).

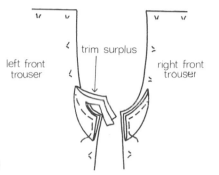

fig 90

On ladies' trousers this may be bulky with some fabrics, so an alternative is to stitch a piece of seam tape into the crutch seam from the inside leg to the base of the zip (fig 91).

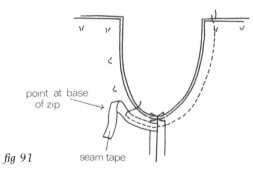

fig 91

Stitch and press open the inside and outside leg seams. If the pattern being used has a shorter back inside leg seam than front, stretch this edge under the iron first so that it becomes the same length as the front seam. This produces better shaped trousers.

Trouser Creases

Press creases into trousers before joining the legs together. Even at the fitting stage the trousers will look better with creases already in. Press them on a table, as an ironing board is not wide enough to press legs in one operation. Take care to cover the table with a cloth as heat can damage the table's surface.

Arrange one trouser leg on the table with the hem to the right and the inside leg seam uppermost. Move this seam slightly towards the front of the trouser, about 2 cm ($\frac{3}{4}$ in), so that the inside and outside leg seams are not on top of each other but running parallel this distance apart up to the crutch. Smooth out the fabric so that the leg is lying flat. Begin pressing at the hem on the front crease. Use a hot iron and a damp cloth to press in the crease from the hem, up the leg, for about two lengths of the iron (fig 92). (For the sake of clarity, the damp muslin is not shown under the iron in the illustration.)

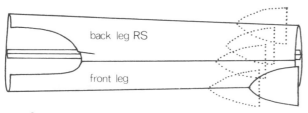

fig 92

Remove the cloth and bang in the steam with a pressing block. Press from the front crease across the leg to the back, the back crease finding its own position. Remove the cloth and bang (fig 93).

Return to the front crease and press another section, then press across the leg to form the back crease. Continue in this way until you are within

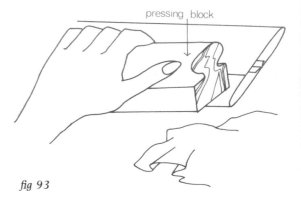

fig 93

15 cm (6 in) of the trouser fork or crutch. From that point there is fulness across the inside leg area, so you cannot press across the leg. Continue pressing the front crease right up to the waist.

On men's trousers the crease runs into the front pleat. On ladies' trousers the crease runs to a point about 6 cm ($2\frac{1}{2}$ in) from the centre front, but not necessarily to meet the front dart. The dart may be moved or even removed at fitting, but the crease must still be in its correct position.

Next return to the back crease and complete it. This one must finish exactly at the centre back. You will find that you will have to rearrange and manipulate the trouser in order to achieve this. Turn the leg over and press the lower leg section again. Hang the trouser leg up to cool. Press the second trouser leg in the same way.

Linings

Loose linings

A loose lining in a dress or skirt is added for comfort, and it prolongs the life of the garment. It will not prevent creasing or seating (see page 49 on mounting for this). The lining is inserted near the end of the garment construction; it can even go in after the hem has been turned up.

Cut out the lining using the pattern pieces, but omitting areas where facings occur. Remember to add turnings to the lining where you are leaving off a facing. Cut out slightly outside the pattern edge all round to allow ease, because most lining fabrics have no give in them. The exception to this would be if nylon jersey were being used as a lining.

Tack up the lining and try it on, making any adjustment you made on the garment when it was fitted. Stitch the lining seams and press open. Neaten the raw edges. Remember that the side towards the body will be the RS.

Skirt

Place the lining in a skirt before attaching the waistband but after inserting the zip. Put the edges of the skirt and the lining together at the waist, and baste. Also baste at the seams (fig 94).

Attach the waistband. Turn under the edge of the lining by the zip and hem. Turn up the lining hem so that it is about 3 cm ($1\frac{1}{4}$ in) shorter than the skirt. At the hem, work bar tacks (french tacks) at the side seams and at the centre front and centre back. Make the tacks 5 cm (2 in) long (fig 95).

Pleats

When lining a pleated skirt, make a seam in the lining where the pleat comes, and stitch the seam

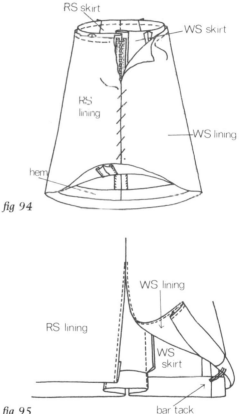

fig 94

fig 95

down to just below the level of the pleat. Leave the seam open below this. At the hem work bar tacks at the seams only, not where the pleats fall.

Dress

Make up the lining. Match up the shoulder seams of the lining and dress, and baste. It is a good idea to use a dress dummy for this if you have one. Baste round the neck and armholes and down the seams (fig 96).

43

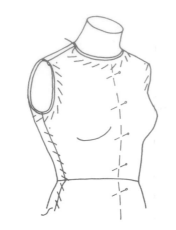

fig 96

Turn in and tack the neck edge of the lining (this may be taken right up to the neck edge, eliminating a neck facing which can be bulky). Fell the lining round the neck, prick stitch along the shoulders, taking stitches right into the garment seams, and prick stitch down the side seams as far as the waist (fig 97).

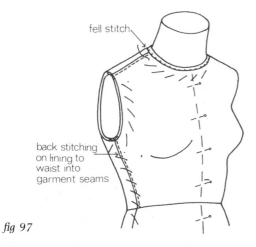

fell stitch

back stitching on lining to waist into garment seams

fig 97

On a sleeveless dress, turn in the lining edges, and fell a little way back from the armhole edge. Turn up the hem so that it is 3 cm (1¼ in) shorter than the dress. Work bar tacks at intervals. Narrow matching lace may be attached to the hem of the lining.

Sleeves

Short sleeves
Stitch the dress and lining seams, and press. There is no need to neaten the edges. Put the sleeve and the lining RS together, tack round the lower edge,

and machine. Trim the seam, turn the lining through, roll the lower edge, tack and press. When rolling make sure the lining is a little back from the sleeve edge. Smooth the lining over the sleeve, pulling it up well so that it will not drop in wear and show at the hem. Baste the two layers round the sleeve head (fig 98).

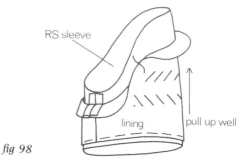

RS sleeve

lining   pull up well

fig 98

Set the sleeve to the armhole, leaving out the lining. Back stitch the lining turnings to the armhole turnings (fig 99). Turn the sleeve edge of the lining over, and bring it onto the armhole turnings. Tack and fell. (See page 37 for illustrations.)

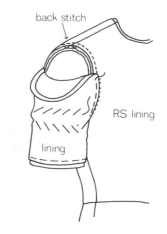

back stitch

RS lining

lining

fig 99

Long sleeves
Match the ws of the back sleeve head to the ws of the back sleeve lining (fig 100).

Back stitch the lining turnings to the sleeve turnings (see page 47 for the illustration). Turn the sleeve through to bring the lining over the sleeve. To do this, insert the hand through the lining from the hem and grasp the head of the sleeve lining that is lying uppermost. Pull the

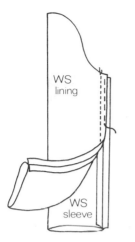

fig 100

lining down until the sleeve is *all* inside the lining (fig 101).

Baste the lining to the sleeve. At the wrist, finish the hem of the sleeve, then turn under the

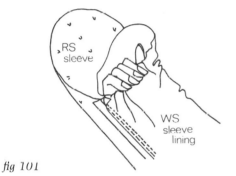

fig 101

lining edge so that it falls about 1.5 cm ($\frac{5}{8}$ in) back from the bottom of the sleeve. Draw back the lining a little further to add ease in the length for bending the arm. Tack and fell (fig 102).

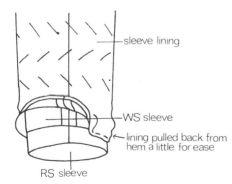

fig 102

Set the sleeve into the armhole, omitting the linings. Back stitch the armhole lining turnings to the dress armhole, then bring the sleeve lining edge over and fell (see page 48 for illustration).

Lining a coat or jacket

Cutting out

Use the pattern pieces, but place the back against the fold of the lining 1.5 cm ($\frac{5}{8}$ in) from it to allow a pleat. If a back neck facing is given in cloth, do not use it, but cut the back lining up to the neck. Cut the front linings minus the front facing. For all pieces, cut a little outside the edge, as the lining must be bigger than the garment (figs 103, 104).

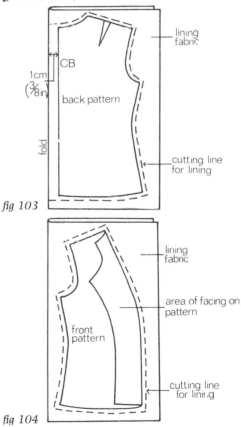

fig 103

fig 104

Assembling

Stitch and press any darts or tucks. If you have a separate pattern for the lining it may well suggest tucks in some places instead of darts. Tack in the pleat in the centre back of the lining. On a jacket, stitch the pleat on the ws from the hem to just above the waist. On a full length coat it helps in providing ease to leave the pleat tacked right to the hem. Press the pleat to one side (fig 105).

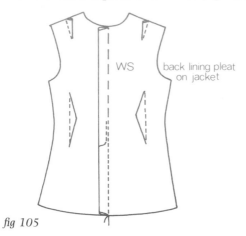

fig 105

In a man's jacket, front linings are first joined to the cloth facings to enable the inside pocket to be made. The facings are then joined to the coat at the front edge (see page 31). Where the raw edge of this seam falls on the canvas, back stitch or flash baste the turnings to the canvas. Also tack the turnings together at the side front seam (fig 106).

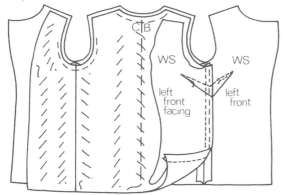

fig 106

In a lady's coat there is no need to seam the front lining to the facing, so the facing can be attached and finished on its own, and the lining side seams joined. Stitch the width of the needle outside the fitting line to allow ease. Press the turnings towards the front.

Line up the centre back pleat against the centre back of the coat and baste from below neck to above hem. Smooth out the lining as far as the side seams and work another row of basting either side of the centre, down through the dart if there is one. Baste across the back neck and round the armhole keeping at least 3 cm ($1\frac{1}{4}$ in) inside the edge, and baste down beside the side seam. Avoid basting where the shoulder pads will be placed.

On a lady's coat back stitch or flash baste the lining turnings to the coat turnings. Start at least 3 cm ($1\frac{1}{4}$ in) below the armhole. Smooth out the front linings on the lower half of the coat and work a couple of rows of basting from the hem up to the bust shaping. Then lift the top of the coat onto your hand, smooth the lining over the bust, and baste in the centre up to the shoulder. Baste round the armhole and down the front edge.

Finishing

Hold the lining in place by working a row of basting along the hem 5 cm (2 in) from the edge. Do this from the RS of the jacket (fig 107).

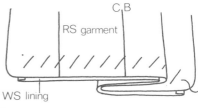

fig 107

Turn in all raw edges round the hem and front edges or side seams, folding under the raw edge before pulling it back slightly, about 3 mm ($\frac{1}{8}$ in) to tack it down. Do not draw the lining back when tacking round the front corners of a lady's coat, nor on a man's coat for the first 5 cm (2 in) of lining beside the facing. At the hem, 1 cm ($\frac{3}{8}$ in) of hem should show on a jacket, 2.5 cm (1 in) on a full length coat (fig 108).

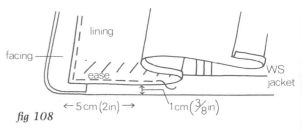

fig 108

Note that on a lady's full length coat you may prefer to finish the lining hem separately, leaving it hanging loose from the coat and attached only at the seams with 2 cm ($\frac{3}{4}$ in) bar tacks.

Finally finish the shoulders and collar (see page 62).

Finishing neck and shoulders
Smooth the front lining up to the shoulder and back stitch the lining edge to the shoulder seams, or to the shoulder pads (fig 109).

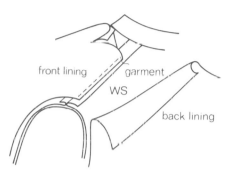

fig 109

Smooth the back lining up so that it falls over the front shoulder. Turn under the raw edge of the lining across the back of the neck, including the pleat, and tack down (fig 110).

Turn under and tack the lining edges across the shoulder. Fell across the shoulders and the back neck, hemming down the edge of the pleat for 2 cm ($\frac{3}{4}$ in).

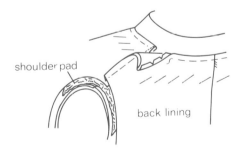

fig 110

Braid or piping
Folded crossway strips of lining or contrasting fabric may be inserted under the edges of the lining before felling to the fabric (fig 111).

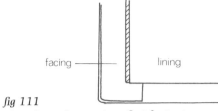

fig 111

Another decorative finish is to complete the felling, then hem a narrow decorative braid over the edge (fig 112).

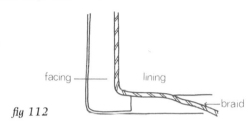

fig 112

Sleeve linings

Tack and machine the under sleeve seam. Stitch the width of the needle outside the fitting line to allow ease. Press towards the back. Tack and machine the top seam, matching balance marks to ease in any fulness. Stitch just outside the fitting line. Press to one side.

Have sleeves and linings ws out and place the turning of the under sleeve seam against the same seam on the sleeve. Be sure to put the right lining to the appropriate sleeve. Using a long back stitch, attach the lining turnings to the sleeve turnings on both under and upper sleeves. End the back stitch 5 cm (2 in) below the sleeve head and 12 cm ($4\frac{3}{4}$ in) above the cuff (fig 113).

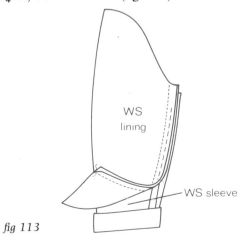

fig 113

Draw the lining through by putting your hand through the wrist and up to the sleeve head; take hold of the lining and sleeve, and pull through. With the lining now RS out, work a couple of rows of basting through the lining and sleeve to hold the lining in place. Work another row of basting round the top of the sleeve about 4 cm (1½ in) in from the raw edge (fig 114).

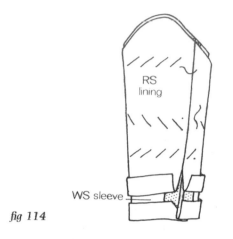

fig 114

Hems

Trim the raw edge of the lining if necessary, turn up the lining so that 2.5 cm (1 in) of sleeve is visible, and crease the lining. Turn under the lining edges beside the cuff opening. On the button side the lining runs level with the edge, on the buttonhole side it slopes in to a point 3 cm (1¼ in) from the edge to allow room for the buttonholes. Tack down, but when working round the hem of the sleeve draw the lining back about 3 mm (1¼ in) to allow ease (fig 115). Finish by felling with small invisible stitches.

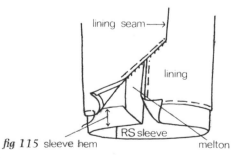

fig 115 sleeve hem   melton

Sleeve heads

Fold back the lining and set in the sleeves (see page 44). Stitch the lining to the armhole (see page 44). Insert shoulder pads (see page 50). Baste back lining over front at shoulders. Arrange coat WS out, but with the sleeve still tucked into the armhole. Start at the centre of the sleeve head and turn under a small turning on the raw edge of the lining (fig 116).

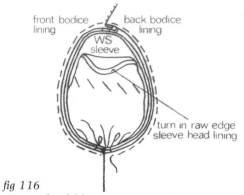

fig 116

Bring the fold over to cover the stitching round the armhole, then pin. Next pin the underarm, then the seams and so on, dividing up the armhole with pins until the lining is in place all round. There will be ease between the pins over the sleeve head and this is folded under as tiny pleats. Tack, then finish with felling (fig 117).

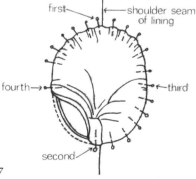

fig 117

To press the sleeves, fold the jacket WS out but with the sleeves still inside the coat; slide the arm-hole onto the sleeve board and press round the underarm. Remove the jacket and turn it RS out; slide it onto the sleeve board and press the body of the coat around the underarm. Then push a pad or rolled towel into the sleeve head, hold it up with one hand while you cover the sleeve head with a damp cloth, and press over the sleeve head join.

Mounting

Mounting, sometimes called underlining, means backing the fabric (before making up) with another material of lighter weight. The effect of this, if it is done correctly, is to support the garment and reduce creasing, produce a better outline, and lengthen the life of the garment. It increases the cost, but it is worthwhile when used on an important item that will be worn for a long time.

What to use
It is essential to choose a mounting fabric that is lighter in weight than the top fabric, otherwise the top fabric will lose its essential nature. The only exception to this might be in a fitted dress in something like chiffon which would obviously need to be mounted onto an opaque fabric.

The choice of mounting fabrics is very limited, but the most useful one for the majority of woven fabrics is Modal/Cotton. Use this to back cottons, moygashel and linen-look fabrics, needlecord, brushed rayon, wool, mixtures and many more. It is also good under pure silk. Modal/Cotton is available on market stalls, and from mail-order fabric firms.

Ordinary lining fabrics can be used as a last resort but they tend to part from the top fabric; they are not very comfortable next to the skin, and some of them split at seams and points of strain. For lighter weight fabrics use polyester voile, cotton voile, triacetate crêpe. For jersey always use nylon jersey.

How to do it
Cut out in fabric, then lift the pieces without removing the pattern, and place them on the mounting fabric. There is no need to pin down. Cut out. Turnings have to be marked, preferably on the mounting as this will be on the WS. This could be done with carbon paper and a tracing wheel. A better but more laborious method is to go ahead and do the mounting and then place all pieces in pairs again, replace the pattern, and tailor tack in the usual way.

Remove the pattern pieces and lay each piece of top fabric onto its mounting. Smooth it out flat on the table and baste together with rows of stitching worked up and down all over the piece. The stitches should be about 4 cm ($1\frac{1}{2}$ in) long and the rows 4 or 5 cm (2 in) apart. Use tacking thread, or, on fine fabrics, use machine-embroidery thread, and not too big a needle or you may leave holes in the fabric (fig 118).

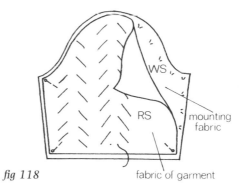

fig 118   fabric of garment

Now make up the garment as usual, treating it as one layer of material. Hems, darts etc should be sewn as usual.

If the garment is to be loose-lined as well (e.g. a coat) the lining is inserted in the usual way.

Shoulders

Shoulder pads

For a coat or jacket

Use thin foam pads and build them up to the required thickness with wadding. These pads do not collapse like the old fashioned ones made entirely from wadding. Vary the amount of wadding if one shoulder is lower than the other on the figure (fig 119).

fig 119

For a normal shoulder place a thin layer of wadding on each side of the pad and baste through all layers with tacking thread. Place in position in the coat, trim off any surplus along the armhole edge and back stitch to the armhole turnings (fig 120).

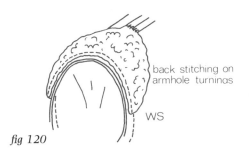

back stitching on armhole turnings

WS

fig 120

For a dress or unlined jacket

A small foam pad is usually sufficient for a dress

but if the figure needs it, the pad can be built up as described above.

Cover the pads by cutting two pieces of lining for each, larger than the pad. Wrap one piece round the pad over the top and pin all raw edges to the under side of the pad (fig 121).

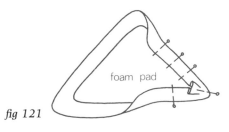

foam pad

fig 121

Place the second piece of lining on the under side, turn in the edges and pin all round. Hem the folded edge all round the pad (fig 122).

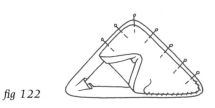

fig 122

Fold the pad not quite in half and have the larger half to the back, with the edge level with the armhole edge. Insert by placing in position and working bar tacks 5 cm (2 in) long. Place one at each end of the pad, one a little longer at the centre, and one at the outside edge attaching it to the shoulder seam (fig 123).

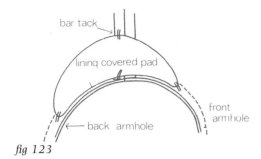

fig 123

Sleeve head roll

This is an additional fold of soft fabric, such as domette, tailor's felt or lambswool, put in the head of the sleeve to keep it in shape and prevent it from collapsing in wear.

Fold the fabric on the cross, and cut a banana shape about 5 cm (2 in) wide at the centre and 25 cm (10 in) long.

After inserting the sleeve and shoulder pad fold back the top of the sleeve head and back stitch the roll to the turnings of the armhole. Put the fold level with the raw edges, arrange some ease over the head, and back stitch to the turnings. When the sleeve head is pressed, the fabric on both sides of the back stitching is pressed out into the sleeve head to support it (fig 124).

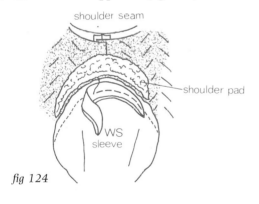

fig 124

Zip Openings

Inserting a zip fastener

The aim is to insert the zip into the garment in such a way that it cannot be seen from the outside. A concealed zip is specially made and is totally invisible when inserted, but with other types of zip some care is needed in preparation and stitching. Hand sewing often produces a better result, as the 'push' of the machine on the fabric is avoided, as is the pressure of the machine on the fabric which can cause a deep, obvious dent, especially on some delicate fabrics.

If you stitch by hand, use prick stitch, the invisible back stitch. Use short pieces of thread, and take the needle back into the work a fraction behind where it emerges; take the needle under for the shortest possible distance, certainly no more than 5 mm ($\frac{3}{16}$ in). Though small, this stitch is usually strong enough to hold a zip, but if you feel the zip needs additional strength, a row of machining can be worked through the turning and the edge of the tape.

Even hems insertion

With this method the fabric tends to pull off the zip when stitched and reveal the teeth, so that part of the seam where the zip is to go must be stitched up. Do this by stitching the seam up beforehand with a large machine stitch (fig 125), and then pressing the seam open (fig 126).

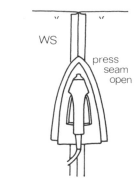

fig 126

Alternatively, turn in, tack and press the edges, place them over the zip with the folds meeting (fig 127), and tack and oversew the folds together before sewing in the zip (fig 128).

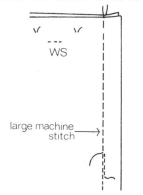

fig 125

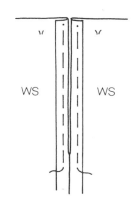

fig 127

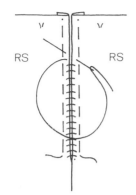

fig 128

Stitching straight across the base of the zip usually produces a bubble of fabric at that point; it is better to work two rows of stitching without sewing across the base or, where strength is needed (e.g. on trousers) sew to a 'V' (figs 129, 130).

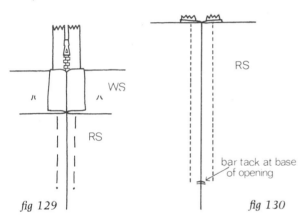

fig 129   *fig 130*

bar tack at base of opening

Uneven hems insertion

In this method the two edges are of uneven width to ensure that the teeth remain covered by the wider hem. The seam line must be clearly marked because you can add to concealment by putting the zip not on the seam line but 2 or 3 mm ($\frac{1}{8}$ in) beyond it, further inside the opening.

Do not stitch up the part of the seam where the zip is to go. Decide which is to be the wider hem and turn it in on the seam line. Tack and press.

Place the zip RS down onto the other turning edge with the teeth over the seam line; tack close to the teeth and stitch. This could be done by machine as the stitching will not show, and since only one layer of fabric is being sewn through, it is not bulky (fig 131).

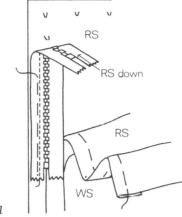

fig 131

Fold the zip over so that it is RS up, then roll the fabric from the edge and tack close to the zip. Press up to the teeth, using the toe of the iron (fig 132).

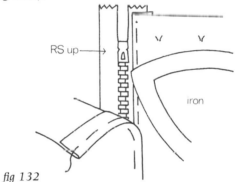

fig 132

Place the top piece or wider hem over the zip, lining up the fold over the tacking beside the teeth. Keeping that fold in position for the whole length of the zip, tack beside the teeth. Oversew the fold to the garment to prevent it from slipping. Stitch the zip, preferably by hand (fig 133).

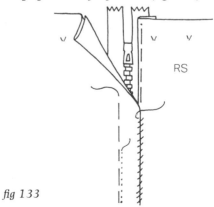

fig 133

Finishing the top of the zip can be difficult where attaching a facing. One method of simplifying this is to attach the neck facing to the wide hem side only, before turning it in and tacking. Keeping the facing extended, turn in, tack, and press the edge (fig 134).

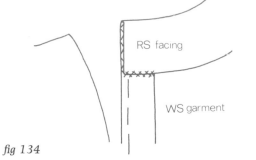

fig 134

Fold the facing onto the ws, tack, press, and slip stitch the folded edges together (fig 135).

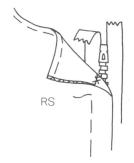

fig 135

On the narrow hem side attach the facing across the top of the zip (fig 136).

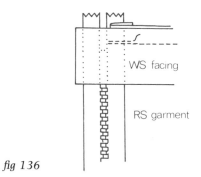

fig 136

Turn in the end of the facing, fold it to the ws. Tack and hem beside the zip. Hem along the lower edge of the facing where it crosses the seam turning and zip tape (fig 137).

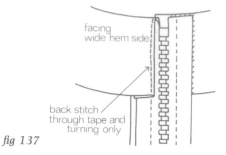

fig 137

Concealed zip

This is the easiest type of zip to insert as no stitching shows on the RS of the garment. Begin by closing the section of seam where the zip is to go with large machine stitches. Press open. It will be advantageous to make the opening 1 cm ($\frac{3}{8}$ in) shorter than the length of zip (fig 138).

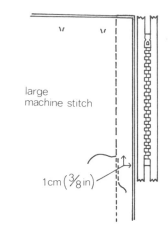

fig 138

Place the zip RS down on the ws of the closed opening with the teeth exactly over the seam. Slide your fingers under the turning, hold the tape steady on the turnings and tack. The tacking is done through the tape and the turning, but not through the garment. Tack both sides (fig 139).

Remove the big machine stitches and open the zip. It is now possible to roll the teeth out and stitch close to them. If the stitching is not close beside the teeth then the tape will show on the RS. Back stitch by hand, or machine, down each side as far as possible. The slider will prevent you from stitching right to the bottom of the tape. Fasten off the stitching (fig 140).

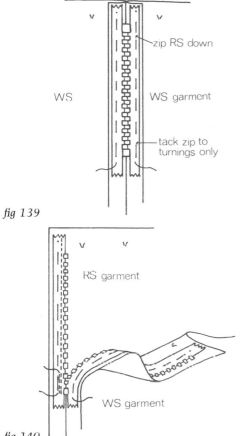

fig 139

fig 140

Close the zip and stitch the bottom part of the tape and turning. This stitching is slightly further away from the teeth, but keep it as close as possible (fig 141).

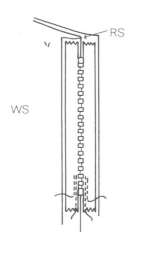

fig 141

Points to remember

Care taken over the following points will give any zip a better appearance and lengthen its life.

Never pin a zip to fabric, as the zip will snake. The position of the top of the teeth is usually critical, so anchor this with one pin if you must, but then insert the zip by holding it firmly and tacking, easing the fabric onto the tape.

If stitching by machine, use an adjustable one-sided zip foot, sometimes called a piping foot, and place it close up against the teeth.

Always make sure the opening is long enough to take the zip, and that the finished zip opening is long enough for the garment to be drawn onto the wearer with ease. Never economize by using a zip that is slightly too short, for the wearer may need a longer zip than the pattern indicates (e.g. a figure with large hips will require a 23 cm (9 in) zip in trousers and skirts instead of the 20 cm (8 in) zip which is usually recommended).

Work a bar tack at the base of the zip after inserting for additional strength.

If the slider sticks, especially after dry cleaning, do not force it; run a cake of beeswax along the teeth to ease it.

Never press directly on top of a zip. To press the ws place the zip RS down on a folded towel or piece of blanket. To press the RS wrap a damp cloth over the toe of the iron and press alongside the teeth.

Man's trouser zip

The zip in men's trousers is sometimes curved at the bottom to fit the start of the crutch seam curve. This means setting the zip to this seam at the base (normally using a 25 cm (10 in) zip) and then, on reaching the waistband, cutting through the zip to trim off the surplus. The depth of the trouser rise is different on each person, so varying amounts need to be trimmed.

However, the manufacture of curved zips is, apparently, now limited, so a straight, and therefore shorter, zip may have to be used. It must end before the start of the curved part of the seam begins.

Zip – Right side and fly extension

Place the zip RS down to the seam line on the RS of the cloth. Tack, and machine 5 mm (¼ in) from the teeth; fasten off well at the base of the teeth (fig 142).

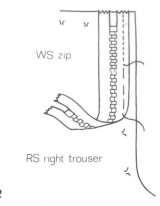

WS zip

RS right trouser

fig 142

Place the fly extension, or guard, RS down on top of the zip, then tack and machine (fig 143).

As this second row should fall on the first row as near as possible, turn the work over and stitch from underneath (fig 144).

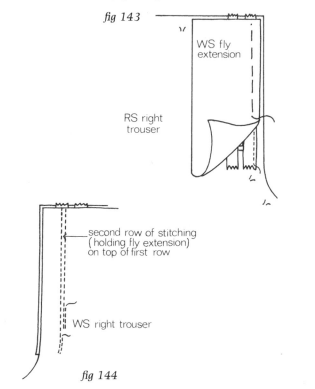

fig 143

WS fly extension

RS right trouser

second row of stitching (holding fly extension) on top of first row

WS right trouser

fig 144

Fold over the guard so that it forms an extension, fold the trouser leg back with RS uppermost, and tack through all the layers beside the teeth.

Cut a piece of silesia or lining to back the guard; make it wider than the guard but long enough to cover the depth of the waistband later. Place this against the fly guard extension WS together, and baste. Turn in, tack, and press the edge of extension. Turn in and hem to it the edge of the silesia leaving the top edge loose to allow the waistband to be attached (fig 145).

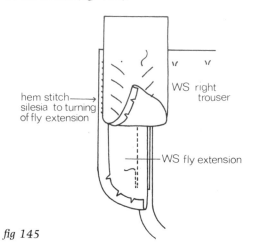

hem stitch silesia to turning of fly extension

WS right trouser

WS fly extension

fig 145

Turn in the other edge of the silesia just beyond the zip and tack down. From the RS, prick stitch beside the zip teeth through all the layers of cloth including the silesia (fig 146).

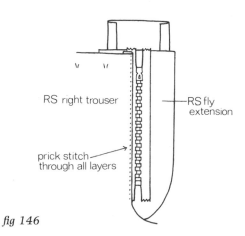

RS right trouser

RS fly extension

prick stitch through all layers

fig 146

6   *Men's trousers showing the zip, waistband and side seam pocket*

Man's trouser waistband

Cut strips of cloth on the straight grain 6 cm (2¼ in) wide and long enough to fit the waist of the trousers. On the right end of the trouser side it must be long enough to include the fly extension plus turnings. On the left end it should include 8 cm (3 in) for overlap plus turnings. Cut firm interfacing (collar canvas or *Vilene*) slightly narrower, and attach. Baste canvas and cloth together (fig 147).

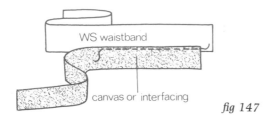

fig 147

Fold over the top edge of the cloth and tack, then herringbone the edge to the interfacing, or with the ws of the band uppermost place the interfacing with one edge just overlapping the cloth, and machine. Fold in the top edge including the interfacing, so that the machine stitching cannot be seen from the RS of the band. Baste the top edge, and press (fig 148).

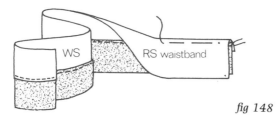

fig 148

Attaching bands

Fold the pocket tops down to prevent them from being caught up in the waistbands. Place the RS of the waistband pieces to the RS of the trouser, tack and machine. The stitching across the top of the zip must be very close to the teeth, so this section may have to be stitched by hand, using double waxed thread and a strong back stitch (fig 149). Press the waist join open.

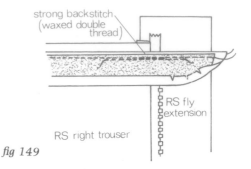

fig 149

Anchor pockets

Replace the tops of the pockets so that they lie flat over the waistband. Trim off the surplus pocket. Back stitch through the pocket and into the waistband join, and then herringbone over the raw edge, picking up only the interfacing (fig 150).

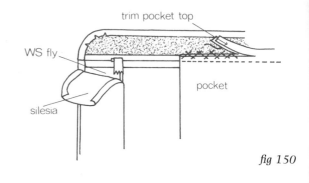

fig 150

Attaching the trouser curtain

Cut pieces of lining on the lengthwise grain 12 cm (5 in) wide and long enough to fit the waistband. Fold in half, and press in the crease. Place inside the trouser with the raw edge just overlapping the waist join. Baste in position (fig 151).

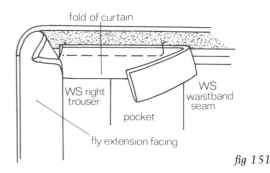

fig 151

On the left side of the trouser, the end of the curtain will tuck under the fly facing. (For strength this can be done before the final prick stitching beside the zip.) At the right side, the trouser curtain tucks under the piece of silesia backing the extension piece. Back stitch the curtain to the waistband along the join. Back stitch across each end of the curtain to the turnings beside the zip. Herringbone over the raw edge of the curtain, taking the stitches through the interfacing only (fig 152).

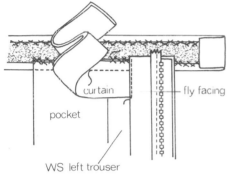

fig 152

Joining the legs

Place the inside leg seams with RS together; place the waistbands exactly together; then tack. Stitch this seam with a strong back stitch using double waxed thread. The reason for hand sewing it is to allow this seam, which is on the cross, to give in wear. It could be machined if a slight zigzag stitch is used, but this will not be as strong as hand sewing.

Stitch through the waistbands, down the seam, under the crutch through the reinforcement and to the base of the zip. Fasten off very firmly.

Press the seam open. I am not in favour of snipping the seam as it weakens it. The seam is not on the straight grain so it should press open easily. Neaten the raw edges by overcasting.

Zip — Left side and flyfacing

Cut the fly facing piece in cloth and also in linen. Baste the linen to the ws of the cloth facing. Place the facing to the trouser, with straight edges and RS together. Machine from the end of the crutch seam stitching up to the waistband. Finish off the stitching firmly at each end. Trim the raw edges, roll the facing to the ws, and baste the edge; then press.

Take the left side of the zip teeth, and place it in position about 1 cm ($\frac{1}{2}$ in) back from the edge of the trouser, or place it so that when the zip is fastened the edge of the fly on the left side covers not only the teeth but also the stitching on the right half of the trouser.

Back stitch the zip to the facing, close to the teeth, then hem along the edge of the tape (fig 153).

Bring the top edge of the facing and zip over the inside of the waistband. Backstitch across the facing, and hem down round the raw edges.

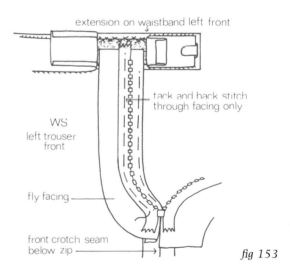

fig 153

On the RS, chalk a line about 3.5 cm ($1\frac{3}{8}$ in) from the finished edge and parallel with it. Curve the line round at the base of the zip to meet the crutch seam. Working with RS up, prick stitch on the line, starting at the waist join.

On reaching the base of the zip, work a small triangle of back stitches right through all the layers, including the guard. Use stab stitch as the area is bulky (fig. 54).

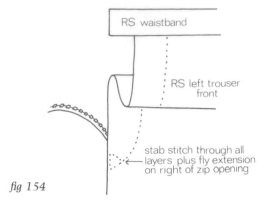

fig 154

Pass the needle through to the ws and stitch through the guard to the turnings at the same point (fig 144), making a strong bar tack (fig 145). Finally stitch the base of the guard to the opened seam turnings.

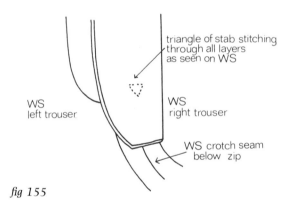

fig 155

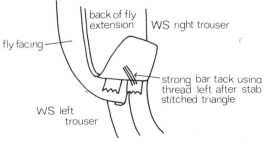

fig 156

Waistlines

Waistband backing

Waistband backing on men's trousers can be a soft backing such as a piece of lining or sleeve lining, or a stiff strong Terylene backing bought by the metre (yard), or a special band backing made of cream knitted nylon with rubber gripping thread running through it, also available by the metre (yard); this latter method eliminates the necessity for a trouser curtain.

Hem the top edge of the backing just below the edge of the waistband. Turn in the ends and hem (fig 157). Turn in the lower edge and hem; if it is a commercial kind with a fold or a selvedge, back stitch through this into the waistband join.

At the centre back seam, lay one side of the curtain and band backing flat over the seam, then lay the second side over it, turn under the raw edge and hem (fig 158).

Where the curtain crosses a dart or seam, work a bar tack at its lower edge to prevent it from rolling up in wear.

Waistline stay

This is useful in a waisted dress for holding the waist in place, especially for loose-fitting blouson or gathered styles. Insert the stay when the dress is complete.

Take a length of curved petersham to fit the waist plus overlap and turnings. Decide how it is to be fastened before cutting. It can be fastened end to end with a large hook and eye, in which case no overlap is needed, or a piece of *Velcro* can be used, in which case the length will be waist plus 7 cm ($2\frac{3}{4}$ in) plus two turnings. (*Velcro* is a touch fastener consisting of two tapes, one of which is covered with tiny nylon hooks, and the other with nylon fuzz; when pressed together they fasten, when pulled apart they are released.) Turn in the two ends of petersham and hem by hand or hold down with a small zigzag stitch. Attach the fastening so that it fits the waist.

Pin to the waist evenly attaching the shorter curve of the petersham to the waist turnings. The fastening should come under the zip. Work bar tacks at intervals to hold, one at each dart and seam and one at the centre front (fig 159).

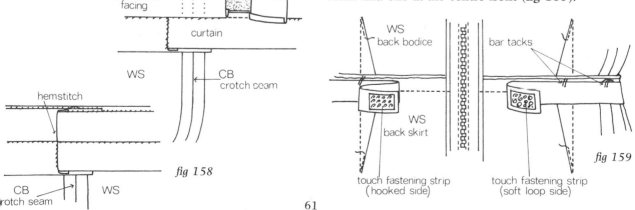

fig 157

hemstitch

waistband facing

curtain

WS

CB
crotch seam

hemstitch

fig 158

CB
crotch seam   WS

WS
back bodice

bar tacks

WS
back skirt

touch fastening strip
(hooked side)

touch fastening strip
(soft loop side)

fig 159

Collars

Tailored coat or jacket collar

The under collar should be cut from melton cloth and stiffened with collar canvas. Cut the canvas on the cross (it is often sold like this). It may need a centre back seam, in which case lap one piece over the other and zigzag stitch together. Seam the melton at the centre back with an open seam trimmed down very narrow. Baste both the melton and the collar canvas together. Mark the roll line with basting.

Padding
Fold the collar, canvas outwards, along the roll line and press the crease with the iron, pulling the collar round into a curved shape (fig 160).

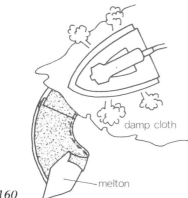

fig 160

With the melton side towards you, work a row of back stitches along the roll line, pulling the thread tight and taking the stitches through to the canvas; pass the needle through to the other side, and work a row of padding stitches over the back stitching (fig 161).

Working with the collar folded on the roll line

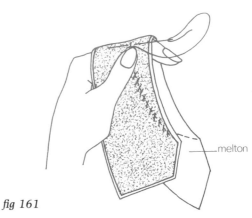

fig 161

and holding the stand part of the collar in your left hand (if right handed), continue padding from the roll line to the neck edge. There will be space for about three rows of padding. Do not work too near the edge of the canvas (fig 162).

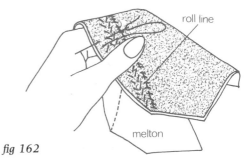

fig 162

Turn the collar round and hold the outer edge. Work rows of padding from the roll line almost to the edge. Holding the collar like this makes it roll under as you stitch; the melton also becomes taut on the canvas, which gives a good shape to the under collar (fig 163). Trim the canvas back 5 mm ($\frac{1}{4}$ in) from the edge of the melton.

7   *Two-piece outfit showing tailored collar and revers, piped buttonholes, and knife pleats*

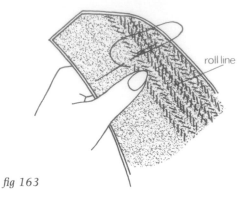

fig 163

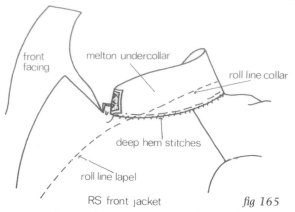

fig 165

Press the under collar with a hot iron and damp cloth. Press up to the roll line on each edge on both the ws and rs of the collar. Stretch the outer edge at the centre back, and the inner edge at the centre back, under the iron to curve the collar. If you are not sure of the correct shape for the collar, it can be put round the neck of a dummy and pressed. Try not to stretch the step of the collar up to the shoulder line at this stage.

Trim the turnings off the under collar pattern, and place it on the collar. Trim the outer edge of the canvas about 2 cm ($\frac{3}{4}$ in) shorter than the melton. This checking is vital because the collar easily becomes distorted while padding and pressing, but it must now be accurately shaped as it forms the base of the top collar.

Attaching the under collar

Place the neck edge of the melton exactly onto the fitting line on the outside of the jacket neck (fig 164).

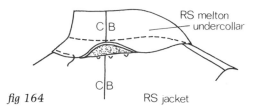

fig 164

Match up the centre back lines and roll lincs and bring the front corners of the melton exactly to the snip at the gorge. Hem the edge of the melton with very small, close, deep stitches. The stitches should catch the canvas along the gorge line (fig 165).

Hem the jacket turnings to the under collar across the back of the neck. Herringbone over the edge of the canvas along the gorge line. Continue the bridle that is left at the top of the lapel roll round the collar. Baste, then hem firmly to the canvas. Press the neck seam, taking care not to pull the collar out of shape. Attach the front facings. Roll back, and work several rows of basting to hold it in a slightly rolled shape (fig 166).

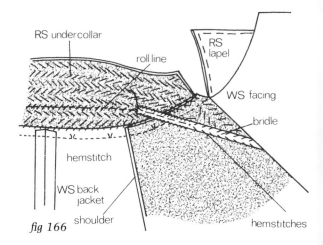

fig 166

Top collar

Placing the top collar in position is easier to do with the jacket on a dummy. Place the top collar ws down onto the under collar, matching the centre backs. Pin at the centre back, the corners, and at the point where the collar meets the lapel. There will be some ease between the pins. Work a row of basting at least 2 cm ($\frac{3}{4}$ in) inside the collar edge, easing in the fulness. With the collar still in its rolled position, work another row of stitches along the roll line (fig 167).

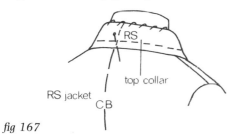

fig 167

Trim the turnings on the collar and facing to 6 mm ($\frac{1}{4}$ in) along the gorge line and also along the step of the lapel, and turn them both in to meet each other (fig 168). Baste in position. Press.

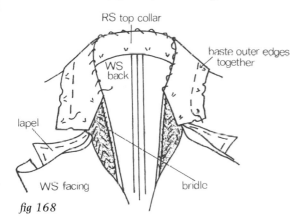

fig 168

Slip stitch or ladder stitch together with tiny deep firm stitches, slightly drawing the two folds together. Slip stitch the step of the lapel (fig 169).

Trim the top edge of the collar to 6 mm ($\frac{1}{4}$ in) beyond the edge of the melton (fig 170).

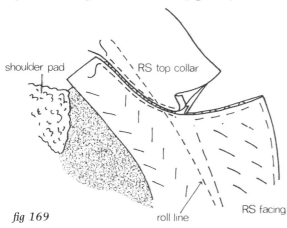

fig 169

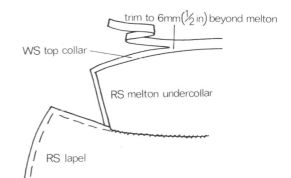

fig 170

Fold over the ends of the top collar, turning the edge in approximately 2 mm ($\frac{1}{16}$ in) wider than the under collar; mitre the corners, cutting away the surplus bulk. Turn in and tack the outer edge of the collar in the same way. Tack the melton down flat to cover the raw edge (fig 171). Press well.

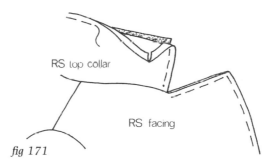

fig 171

If the melton is not a perfect match for the colour of the cloth, it is better to finish the end of the collar in the following way. Turn in the outer edge of the collar, but not the ends. Finish by hemming the edge of the melton. Trim the melton at the collar ends and hem down. Fold the end of the collar over the melton and baste. Hem with tiny stitches along the sides and work over the raw edge with small herringbone stitches. Press well.

This method ensures that the edge of the melton never shows, but in addition it is slightly easier to achieve a well shaped collar end.

Work a bar tack on the underside where the collar and lapel form an angle and hem with tiny, close deep stitches all round the outer edge of the collar.

Finishing the back neck

Tack down the raw edge of the collar below the roll line, then work a row of back stitching from the end of the facing through the top collar and into the melton beneath.

With the collar in its rolled position work another row of back stitching 5 mm ($\frac{3}{16}$ in) below the roll line from the seam of the gorge right across the back of the neck (fig 172). There is a slight amount of ease to be held in place. Complete the back neck of the lining (see page 47).

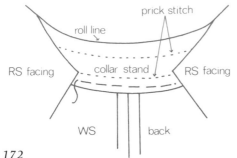

fig 172

If correctly held and padded, the lapel will automatically adopt the correct rolled position. Never press in a crease down the lapel, but press the ws and the rs and, while still damp and warm, roll and fold it back with your fingers, smoothing it until cool.

Semi-tailored coat or dress collar

If it proves impossible to obtain a melton cloth to blend with the fabric, or if you are making a dress where melton would be too heavy, you can compromise and use a method which combines the careful handling and shaping and reduction of bulk of a tailored collar with the necessity of using ordinary fabric for the under collar.

Under collar

Cut the under collar on the cross (there may be a separate pattern piece) and join if necessary at the centre back. Interface. Pad and shape if using canvas; baste or press if using other interfacing such as *Vilene* (fig 173).

Trim off the edge of the interfacing as for a tailored collar. If using sew-in interfacing the edge must be herringboned to the under collar round all edges (fig 174).

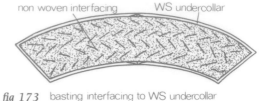

fig 173   basting interfacing to WS undercollar

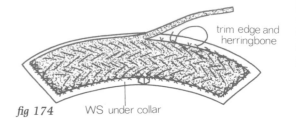

fig 174   WS under collar

Attach the neck edge to the garment, RS together, making sure that the ends of the collar come to the correct points at the front. Snip the edges of the collar and of the neckline to make the join easier to do (fig 175). Tack and machine or back stitch, but only stitch from the centre front mark, do not include the end turnings of the collar (fig 176).

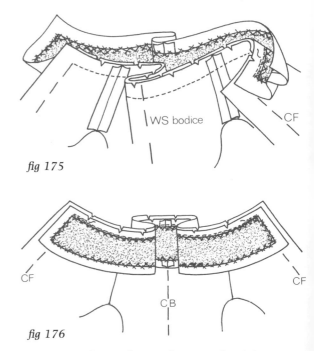

fig 175

fig 176

Remove the tacks, and press the join open, laying it over a pressing pad or rolled up towel (fig 177).

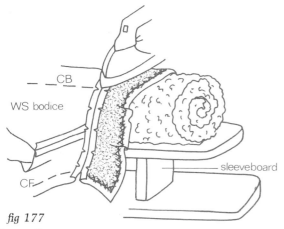

fig 177

Top collar

Place the top collar to the under collar RS together, and tack round the outer edge. Machine round the collar just off the edge of the inter-facing (fig 178).

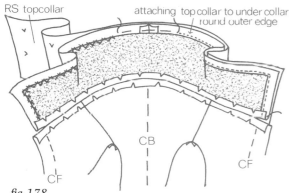

fig 178

Trim and layer the turnings and cut off the corners (figs 179, 180).

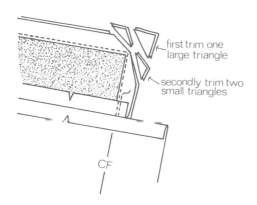

fig 179

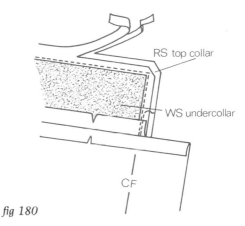

fig 180

Turn the collar through, roll and tack the edges, with the join well concealed on the under side, and press the edge well (fig 181).

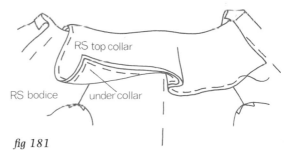

fig 181

Roll the collar into the position it will adopt in wear, and work a row of basting along the roll. Bring the raw edge of the top collar down at the back of the neck and tack (fig 182).

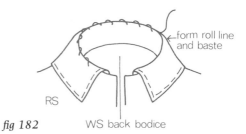

fig 182

Turn the work over and, from the under collar side, work a row of back stitches in the neck join, taking the needle through to the top collar layer. If the garment is not to be lined, neaten the raw edge with overcasting or binding (fig 183).

With a shirt-style collar in a soft fabric, work a row of back stitch across the back of the neck

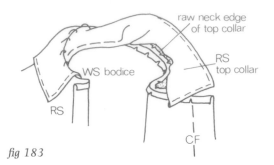

fig 183

1 cm ($\frac{1}{2}$ in) below the roll line. Do not do this on cottons or light-weight fabrics (fig 184).

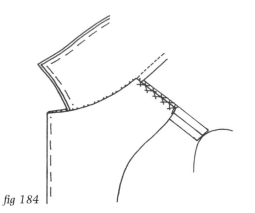

fig 184

Finishing

To finish the revers, open out the front facing, trim the turnings down to 5 mm ($\frac{1}{4}$ in) and turn in the raw edge and tack. Fold the facing over into position and tack. Turn in the raw edge round as far as the shoulder seam and tack. Press. Finish by slip stitching the step of the rever and round to the shoulder with very tiny invisible stitches. Attach the raw edge of the facing at the shoulder with herringbone stitch.

The raw edge of the facing from shoulder to hem can be neatened and left loose on blouses etc, held down with herringbone stitch on heavy fabrics, or it can be held down with pieces of fabric adhesive (such as *Wundaweb*).

Note that this method of applying the under collar first and pressing the neck join open can be used on any fabric and any style of collar. It is easy to manipulate and produces good results. It is better not to use a back neck facing as it adds bulk.

Shirt collar

If a stiff result is wanted, interface the collar, but not if the fabric being used is soft, such as cheese-cloth, muslin or voile.

Interfacing

Interface the under collar and band with a medium-weight iron-on interfacing, but before attaching, cut out a 3 mm ($\frac{1}{8}$ in) wide slit exactly on the roll line. Press in position (fig 185).

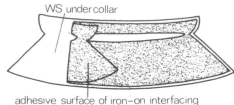

fig 185

Using a firm iron-on interfacing, cut shapes to fit the band and the collar points, and iron into position (fig 186).

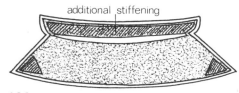

fig 186

Cut off the corners. If the turnings are likely to show through the top collar, or if the fabric is pale or soft, interface the top collar with a fine iron-on interfacing (such as Transparent Vilene).

Making the collar

Place the two collar pieces RS together and machine round the outside on the fitting line. Trim the turnings very narrow, and also layer them. Cut the corners right away. If the band is cut all in one with the collar, snip well round the curved section. Turn to the RS, roll the edge, tack, and press well. If there is a separate band, work edge stitching round the collar first and then attach the band sections. Trim the edges and turn the band pieces to the RS; tack and press.

Attaching the collar

Place the RS of the top collar to the WS of the neck edge; line up the centre fronts and the centre back accurately, and tack. If may help to snip the turnings. Machine from the collar side from the collar stitching one end to exactly the same spot on the other end. Trim the turnings and press into the collar. Turn under the raw edge of the under collar and bring it down onto the machining. Tack. Machine along this edge. If the band is separate, machine round all sides of the band. If the collar and band are cut in one, machine all round the outer edges of the collar and across the back of the neck (fig 187).

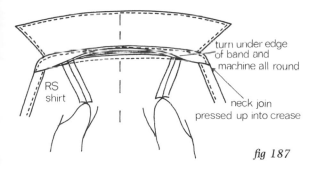

turn under edge of band and machine all round

RS shirt

neck join pressed up into crease

fig 187

Sleeve Openings

The choice of sleeve opening depends very much on the structure of the rest of the garment, for example, whether machine stitching is used for decoration, and also on the type of fabric.

Seam opening

This is a 7 cm (2¾ in) slit left in the bottom of the underarm seam. The cuff is fastened invisibly at the inside of the arm with press studs or a touch fastener (such as *Velcro*). Stitch the seam, leaving the opening, and fastening off the stitching; neaten the turnings and press open. Hold back the turnings of the slit with small pieces of fabric adhesive (such as *Wundaweb*) (fig 188).

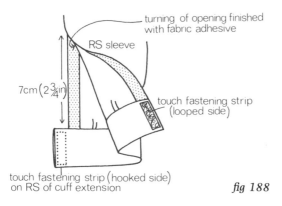

fig 188

Gap-in-sleeve opening

This should be used only on a full gathered sleeve, as the opening then mingles with the gathers. Make two snips 1.5 cm (⅝ in) deep and 2 cm (¾ in) apart in line with the little finger line on the sleeve. This is the usual place for the sleeve opening (fig 189).

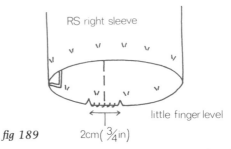

fig 189   2cm(¾ in)

Overcast this little piece of raw edge between the slits (fig 190), press, and hold it back with a small piece of fabric adhesive (such as *Wundaweb*) (fig 191).

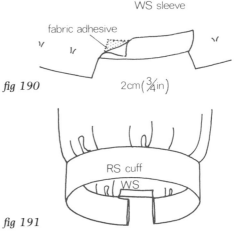

fig 190   2cm(¾in)

fig 191

Hemmed opening

This is rather weak at the top and should only be used on very light-weight fabrics. Cut a 7 cm (2¾ in) slit in the sleeve. Turn in a narrow hem, opening the slit out straight, and hem. The hem becomes very narrow at the top of the opening (fig 192).

70

fig 192

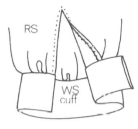

Then attach the cuff in the normal way (fig 193).

fig 193

Faced slit opening

This can be used on any fabric. Cut pieces of fabric 6 × 3 cm ($2\frac{1}{4}$ × $1\frac{1}{4}$ in), and neaten the two long edges and one short one (fig 194).

Press a narrow strip of paper-backed adhesive (such as *Bondaweb*) to the ws (fig 195).

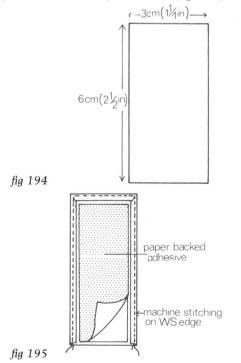

←—3cm($1\frac{1}{4}$in)—→

6cm($2\frac{1}{2}$in)

fig 194

paper backed adhesive

machine stitching on WS edge

fig 195

Tear off the paper. Place the piece RS down to the RS of the sleeve where the opening is to be. Mark the centre of the piece as a guide to stitching (fig 196).

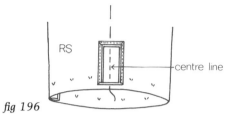

RS

centre line

fig 196

Machine two parallel rows of stitching 5 cm (2 in) long, tapering to a point at the top (fig 197).

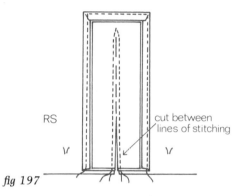

RS

cut between lines of stitching

fig 197

Cut up between the stitching, right to the point. Turn the patch to the ws of the roll, and tack the edge and press well. The adhesive holds the patch in position and prevents fraying (fig 198).

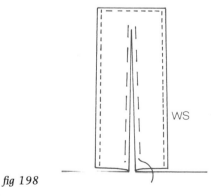

WS

fig 198

Continuous strip opening

This should not be used on bulky fabrics. Cut 6 cm ($2\frac{3}{8}$ in) slits in the sleeves, cut straight strips of fabric 3 cm ($1\frac{1}{4}$ in) wide and 12 cm ($4\frac{3}{4}$ in) long. Open out the slit until it is straight and place the strip RS down to the RS of the sleeve. Tack, taking a turning of 5 mm ($\frac{1}{4}$ in) evenly all along the strip, but allowing the sleeve turning to become very narrow at the centre. Machine from the sleeve side to make sure of catching in a couple of threads at that point. Press the strip upwards with the toe of the iron. Fold over the strip twice and bring the fold onto the machining. Hem into the machining to finish.

Shirt sleeve opening

Cut a slit 10 cm (4 in) long in the sleeve. Turn a narrow hem on the edge nearest the underarm of the sleeve and machine it. Cut a strip on the straight grain 13 cm (5 in) long and 7 cm (2$\frac{3}{4}$ in) wide. Place the strip RS down to the WS of the sleeve against the other side of the slit. Press the strip upwards. Snip into the corner of the stitching on the sleeve. Turn under the other edge and bring it down to cover the machining. Turn under the end of the strip and tack down. Machine along the edge of the strip, across the top and down the other side to a point 1 cm ($\frac{3}{8}$ in) below the slit; turn and machine across the slit to form a rectangle.

Man's shirt sleeve opening

Make sure the opening in a man's shirt sleeve is quite long, to enable the sleeves to be rolled up.

Cut the opening and make a small 3 mm ($\frac{1}{8}$ in) snip at the top at right angles (fig 199).

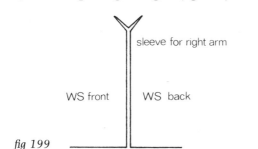

fig 199

Cut a strip of fabric on the straight grain, longer than the slit and 5 cm (2 in) wide. Place this to the WS of the sleeve, against the raw edge at the back of the sleeve. Machine from the end of the slit to the wrist, taking 3 mm ($\frac{1}{8}$ in) turnings (fig 200).

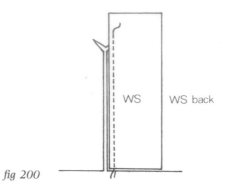

fig 200

Press the strip outwards, roll it to the RS, turn under the edge, baste and machine (fig 201).

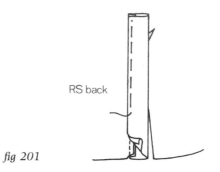

fig 201

Cut a longer strip of fabric 4 cm (1$\frac{1}{2}$ in) wide, place one edge to the raw edge of the slit, with the RS to the WS of the slit. Machine, taking the stitching to the top of the slit (fig 202).

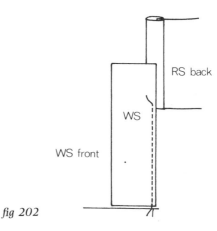

fig 202

Press the join open. Press the strip over to the RS, but allow it to extend 1 cm ($\frac{3}{8}$ in) (fig 203).

Turn in the outer edge of the strip and press. Turn in the top edge of the strip and press (fig 204). This can be made into a point. Press.

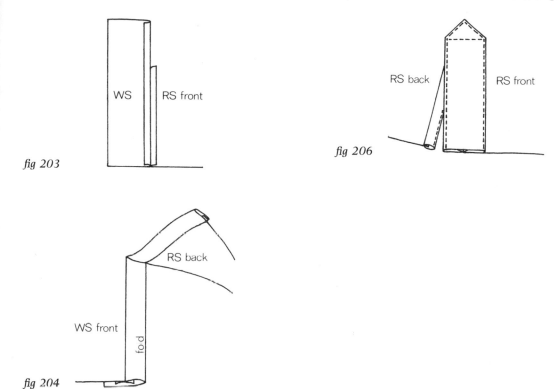

fig 203

fig 206

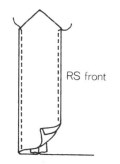

fig 204

Baste the side of the strip to the sleeve, and machine on the edge. Also machine the fold if required (fig 205).

fig 205

Baste the top of the strip to the shirt, making sure that it covers the slit underneath. Machine round the top. Machine across the strip just below the original snip to catch in the underneath strip (fig 206).

Cuffs

Wrap cuff

This avoids the necessity for a sleeve opening, but it is bulky and should only be used on medium and light-weight fabrics.

Interface the cuff. Insert gathering threads in the lower edge of the sleeve. Place the cuff to the sleeve with RS together; pin, and pull up the gathers to fit. Tack and machine from the gathered side. Trim the raw edges, and press them towards the cuff.

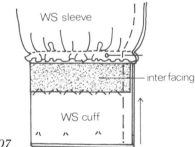

fig 207

Fold the sleeve RS together, and tack the seam. Start at the cuff in order to place the joins exactly level. Place a pin through this join to hold it (fig 207), and machine the whole seam, going slowly over the pin. Press the seam open and neaten the edges of the sleeve section.

Fold and tack the cuff along the fold line. Turn in the raw edge 1.5 cm ($\frac{5}{8}$ in) and tack. Bring the fold onto the machining. Tack and hem into the machining. If you wish to add top stitching, work it now.

The cuff is fastened by making a fold in the position where an opening would normally be, ie in line with the little finger. Pin out the amount to be folded so that the cuff fits. Hem a narrow piece of touch fastener (such as *Velcro*) in position, or attach two press studs. Buttons can be sewn on the outside (fig 208).

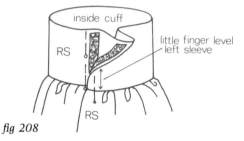

fig 208

Dress cuff

This method is for medium-weight or soft fabrics. Interface the cuff, cutting off the corners of the interfacing to make it easier to turn through. Place the cuff RS down to the RS of the sleeve, allowing an extension on the underside of the sleeve, and making sure that the sides of the opening are the same length. Pin both cuffs to make sure you make a right and a left sleeve. Pull up the gathers to fit. Tack.

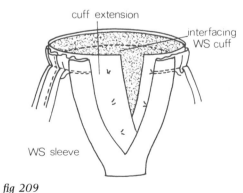

fig 209

Machine from the gathered side (fig 209), stitching exactly from end to end of the sleeve. Remove the tacks and trim the turnings, cutting the cuff edge a little narrower than the gathered edge (fig 210).

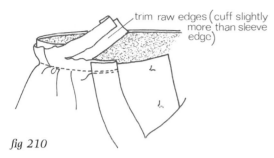

fig 210

Run the toe of the iron along the join between the cuff and the sleeve, but do not flatten the gathers (fig 211).

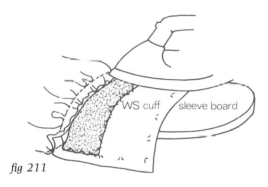

fig 211

Turn in the ends of the cuffs and also the lower edge of the overlap. Tack, press, and trim away some of the raw edge (fig 212).

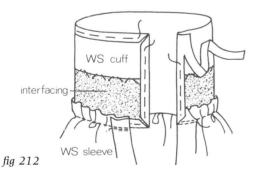

fig 212

Turn in the outer edge of the cuff; tack, press, and trim. Bring this edge down onto the gathers and pin with vertical pins (fig 213).

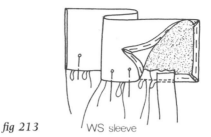

fig 213   WS sleeve

Tack all round the cuff, including the folded edge. Press. Slip stitch the ends and hem into the machining. Remove the tacks (fig 214).

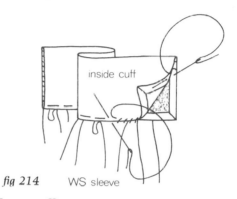

fig 214   WS sleeve

Shirt cuff

The shirt cuff sometimes does not have an overlap as an extension; the cuff simply comes to the edge of the strip of fabric forming the opening.

Interface the cuff and cut off the corners (fig 215).

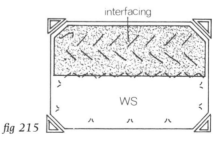

fig 215

Place the cuff RS down to the WS of the sleeve, and pin. Arrange the tucks or gathers, and tack (fig 216).

Machine exactly from end to end of the sleeve (fig 217). Run the toe of the iron along the join between the cuff and the sleeve.

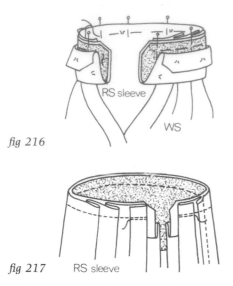

fig 216

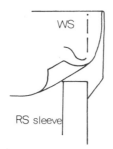

fig 217   RS sleeve

Fold the cuff ends over with RS together, and tack (fig 218).

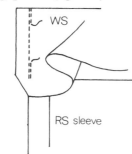

fig 218

Machine across the ends, joining the machining to the row holding the cuff to the sleeve. There must be no gap here (fig 219).

fig 219

Trim the turnings down. Turn the cuff through and roll the edges. Crease the cuff along the folded edges; turn in the raw edge, and bring down to cover the machining. Tack and press. Machine on the fold close to the edge. If desired,

make a second row of stitching all round the cuff, the width of the machine foot, inside the edge.

Fasten the cuffs with buttons and buttonholes, press studs, button snaps or narrow pieces of touch fastener (such as *Velcro*) hemmed into place.

Man's shirt cuff

Cut firm interfacing and attach to the WS of one pair of cuff pieces. Place the interfaced pieces to the backing pieces with RS together. Baste and machine round the outer edge. Trim and layer the turnings (fig 220).

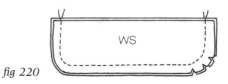

WS

fig 220

Turn the cuff RS out, roll the edges and press.

Baste the pleats into the lower edge of the sleeve and make sure the cuff fits the sleeve exactly, including the underlap formed by the opening.

Place the RS of the cuff (the edge with no inter-facing) to the WS of the sleeve. Pin and baste. Machine, fastening off the ends securely (fig 221).

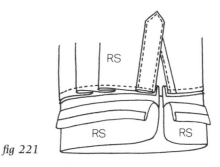

fig 221

Trim the turnings. Bring the outer edge of the cuff up to cover the machine stitching. Turn in the raw edge. Baste down, then press. Machine all round, with two rows of machining if preferred (fig 222). Finally work the buttonholes.

Double cuff

A double cuff is made twice the depth needed. It is attached in the same way as the normal shirt

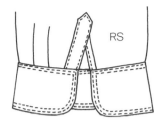

fig 222

cuff, and is folded double after the buttonholes have been worked.

Hole-and-button cuff

Join the top sleeve to the under sleeve at the underarm seam, and press open. If the cloth is soft, as it might be for a lady's coat, reinforce the hem by herringboning a crossway strip of linen or similar. The lower edge must be exactly on the hemline. On the top sleeve, the reinforcement should reach the seam line; on the under sleeve it stops short of the edge by the width of a turning (fig 223).

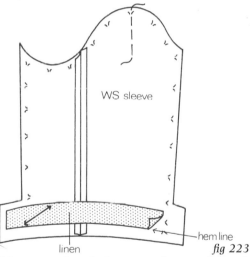

WS sleeve

hem line
linen   *fig 223*

Fold over and tack the raw edge on the under sleeve and fold and tack the extension edge on the top sleeve (fig 224)

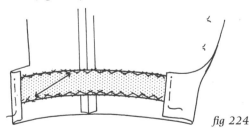

fig 224

Finish by turning up the hem and trimming the corner (fig 225).

fig 225

On a man's coat baste a piece of linen 5×4 cm ($2 \times 1\frac{1}{2}$ in) into each end of the cuff, with the raw edges exactly on the hemline and fold lines (fig 226).

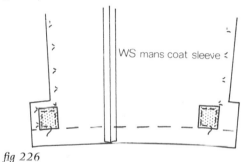

WS mans coat sleeve

fig 226

Tailored hole-and-button cuff

Baste a piece of linen 12 cm ($4\frac{3}{4}$ in) long and 5 cm (2 in) wide to the ws of each side of the sleeve. Stitch the sleeve seam. The depth of the opening depends upon how many buttons are to be used. Press the seam open from the armhole, but towards the front of the sleeve, for about 14 cm ($5\frac{1}{2}$ in) above the opening.

On the underneath or extension side, fold over a single turning, and press. Herringbone to hold.

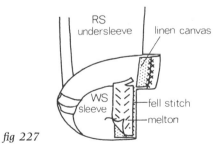

RS
undersleeve   linen canvas

WS
sleeve   fell stitch
    melton

fig 227

8   Man's shirt showing collar and cuffs

On the front side, fold back and press a turning. Cut a piece of melton cloth 6 cm ($2\frac{3}{8}$ in) wide and baste it with its edge to the cuff edge. Fell along this edge. Trim the melton slightly at the top of the opening (fig 227).

Turn up and finish the sleeve hems; mitre the corners over the melton and fell in place.

Lap the opening, and baste it closed from the RS.

On the WS back stitch across the top of the opening through all layers except the sleeve itself. Bring the sleeve lining down. Turn in, and fell close to the edge of the extension piece (fig 228).

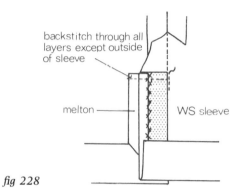

fig 228

On the top side where the buttonholes will go, slope the lining out to reveal the melton. Fell all lining edges (fig 229).

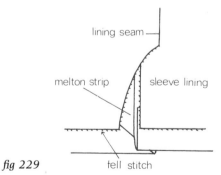

fig 229

Work buttonholes, which need not be actually cut, and attach buttons.

Hems

Dress, coat and skirt hems must be marked by measuring an even distance from the floor. Other hems, on blouses, shirts, sleeves etc, should be trimmed level before turning up. They should be level on the body too. The depth of a hem depends partly on the garment and fabric, and partly on the style.

Narrow machined hem

This hem is used on blouses and shirts and possibly jeans, children's clothes, sleeves and frills.

Turn up a single fold and then turn up again to a depth of between 4 and 6 mm ($\frac{1}{8}$ and $\frac{1}{4}$ in). Tack and press. Work a row of machining close to the fold. If the stitching forms a feature, it looks attractive on some fabrics to work a second row right on the edge. This is particularly effective on plain fabrics. You could work one of the less complicated embroidery stitches on the machine, on both edges or just on the first fold (fig 230).

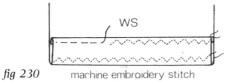

fig 230   machine embroidery stitch

Narrow hand-finished hem

For finer fabrics, the narrow hand-finished hem can be made by turning up and tacking as described above – but making the hem narrower. Press, then slip-hem along the fold. The distance the needle is run through the fold should be no more than 3 mm ($\frac{1}{8}$ in); otherwise the raw edge will spring out (fig 231).

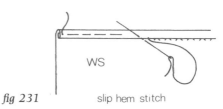

WS

fig 231   slip hem stitch

Narrow hand-rolled hem

Use this hem on very fine fabrics such as silk and georgette. Work a row of straight machine stitching 5 mm ($\frac{3}{16}$ in) below the hem line. Trim very close to the stitching a little at a time, roll the edge over twice, and either whip stitch right over the edge (fig 232), or use small hemming stitches to hold (fig 233). Try both methods to see which looks best. If the fabric is springy or slippery, wet your finger tips to roll the edge.

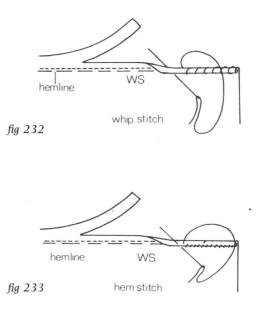

hemline   WS

whip stitch

fig 232

hemline   WS

fig 233   hem stitch

Wide straight hem

This may be needed on children's clothes and can also be used on skirts, coats and dresses. The method of finishing depends on the fabric.

On light-weight cotton fabrics, turn up on the marked hemline, and tack. Press well. Trim down the raw edge to a depth of about 6 cm (2½ in) (it can be even more on children's clothes). Turn under this raw edge and tack down (fig 234). Press again. Finish with slip hemming.

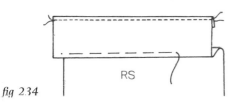

fig 234

If there is a likelihood that the hem will have to be let down at some stage, it helps to machine along the edge of this second fold before tacking down to make the letting down easier.

On thicker fabrics the finishing is different, and so too is the method of tacking up, because most thick fabrics tend to move when handled.

Mark the hemline in the usual way and lay the garment out, RS out, with the hem towards you. Turn up and tack a short stretch across the centre front area. Revolve the skirt, and tack a section at the centre back. Swivel again to tack the area by the side seams. This prevents any 'push', and should lessen the possibility of the hem being off-grain at one side or the other. Press well in short sections on a sleeve board to prevent stretching. Press only the fold.

Trim down the raw edge to a depth of about 5 cm (2 in). Neaten the raw edge. This can be done with a zigzag or overlocking stitch, but both can be harsh and may be inclined to stretch the edge. A better method is to overcast by hand as it gives you the chance to slightly tighten the edge. If the fabric frays, work a row of straight machine stitching below the raw edge; trim close, then overcast over the stitching. Press the stitching.

Tack the neatened edge to the garment. Finish by working catch stitch just under the edge (fig 235). If the fabric is jersey, leave a loop of thread every 5 cm (2 in) or so to take any stretch that

there may be in wear. Remove tacks and press on a sleeve board, placing a piece of spare fabric up against the neatened edge to enable you to press lightly over the whole hem and yet avoid a ridge.

Curved hem

So few fabrics can be shrunk now to remove the fulness from a curved hem that alternative methods must be found.

Turn up, tack, and press the fold. Place the skirt on the table and tack again halfway up the hem depth, easing in some fulness. Trim, then neaten with pulled-up overcasting, and finish.

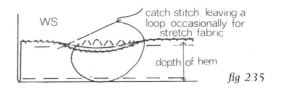

fig 235

If it proves impossible to dispose of all the fulness then sections must be cut out of the hem. (Darts will eventually show.) Smooth the hem out and, where the fulness occurs seriously, cut out a 'V' shape and re-join the edges either with herringbone stitch or (more difficult to manipulate) with a zigzag machine stitch (fig 236).

Trim and neaten the edge, and catch stitch down.

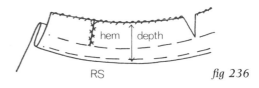

fig 236

Circular hem

Remember to let the skirt hang for a few days before marking the hemline. This is to allow it to drop to its maximum at the points where it is on the cross. Fabric seldom drops evenly, as the warp threads are weaker and tend to stretch more than the weft.

This is probably the most difficult hem of all. Trim the raw edge to within 1 cm (⅜ in) of the marked hemline. Turn a double fold, and tack. Take care not to stretch the areas that are on the cross. Press in short sections on a sleeve board, supporting the rest of the hem beneath. Finish with machining, using a straight, zigzag or decorative stitch, or slip hem by hand.

Coat hem

This hem can be used on garments other than coats, but only on medium to heavy fabrics, as it is inclined to show on others.

Turn up, tack, and press the fold as usual. Do not trim down the raw edge, but make a chalk line 4 cm (1½ in) above the fold. Cut bias strips of lining fabric (joining if necessary); place the RS down to the RS of the hemline, and tack through the chalk line, taking a 5 mm (³⁄₁₆ in) turning on the strip. Machine, remove the tacks, and run the toe of a cool iron along under the strip so that it stands upright. Trim down the fabric edge to 5 mm (³⁄₁₆ in) (fig 237).

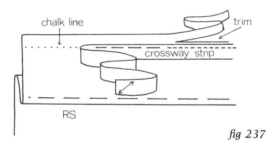

fig 237

Fold the strip over the edge and hold so that it tightly binds the edge. Work a hand prick stitch from the RS through the join to hold the lining down (fig 238). Fig 239 shows the reverse side.

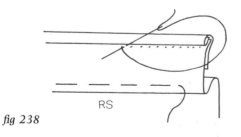

fig 238

Tack the hem flat to the coat and catch stitch. Press carefully using a spare piece of fabric as described for the wide hem (page 81).

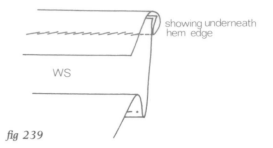

fig 239

Coat lining hem

After turning up the coat hem, trim the lining about 2 cm (¾ in) below the bottom edge of the coat. Turn up a double hem in the lining 4 cm (1½ in) deep when finished. Tack and press. Finish with slip hemming or use the blind hem stitch decoratively, or use an embroidery stitch on the machine.

Coat corners

The same method also applies to any garment other than a coat where there is a conventional wrap-over fastening.

Open out the facing section and turn up the hem. Tack and press (fig 240). Take the tacking right to the front edge; keep the seam open. Check that both front edges are exactly the same length. Trim down the facing and the hem for that part which will fall inside the hem (fig 241). Finish the hem.

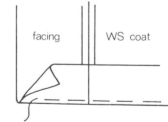

fig 240

Fold the facing into position, fold under the lower edge so that it falls on top of the hem edge but slightly back from it. Tack firmly (fig 242).

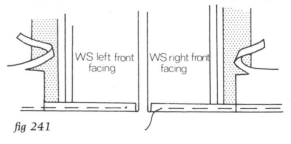

fig 241

Loop stitch with small stitches over the raw edge where it crosses the hem. Slip stitch the two folds together (fig 242). Press well.

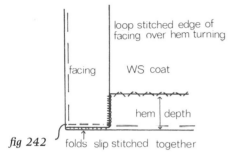

fig 242

Reinforcing hems

If jackets or coats are made from very soft fabric, as women's often are, the sleeve hems and jacket hems needed reinforcing before turning up. This is done with bias strips of tailor's linen, soft canvas, or, on some fabrics, it works well to use interfacing such as light-weight *Vilene*.

The strips should be about 3 cm (1¼ in) wide. Do not join; simply overlap where necessary. Place one edge on the hemline and tack in position from where the interfacing ends at the front. Work catch stitch over each edge, taking only one thread of the garment cloth (fig 243).

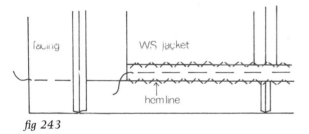

fig 243

Binding

Making crossway and bias strips

Cutting

True cross strips are cut at 45° to the selvedge; take a warp thread and fold the fabric until it lies over a weft thread, so producing a fold on the cross. Cut carefully along this fold and then cut strips parallel with the cut edge (fig 244). Press the strips, stretching them slightly to avoid them bubbling when they are used.

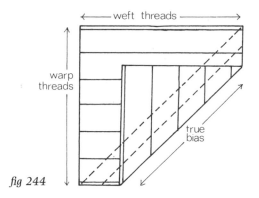

fig 244

Bias strips can be cut slightly off the 45° angle and this can be useful if you are short of fabric. Some fabrics stretch less than others so test a small piece first to make sure there will be enough give for the particular position for which it is needed. Do not stretch the strips as you will need all the give there is in them.

Note that you must cut true cross strips on some fabrics (eg checks) or the pattern will look odd.

Joining

If you have a rectangle of fabric to spare and you need a long piece of crossway fabric, you can make it by joining the piece first and then cutting. First mark out the strips at 45° in the width required (fig 245). Mark with chalk or tacking. Trim off the triangles left at each end (fig 246).

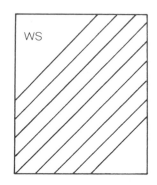

fig 245

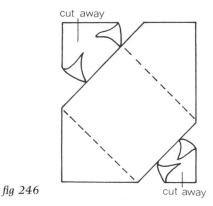

fig 246

Fold the fabric with RS together to join the shorter edges together, but leave the width of one strip extending as you start to tack. Machine a seam and press open (fig 247). Cut the strip by cutting round and round following the chalk line (fig 248).

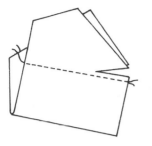

fig 247

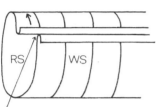

fig 248 begin cutting continuous bias strip here

To join short lengths of crossway strip, place the strips, end to end, WS up, and trim off on the straight grain (fig 249).

Using the iron, press over a small turning on each strip (fig 250).

trim ends of strips on straight of grain   *fig 249*

press each end back in small turnings   *fig 250*

Lift these ends and place the creases together; pin or tack (fig 251).

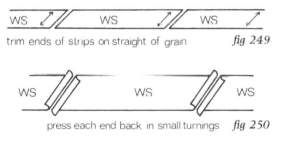

fig 251

Open each join out and look at it from the RS to make sure the long edges are level. Stitch by machine or hand (fig 252).

Press the joins open and trim off the edges (fig 253).

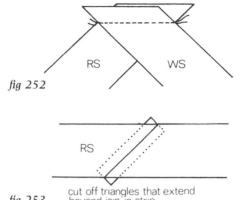

fig 252

fig 253 cut off triangles that extend beyond join in strip

Single binding

Place the crossway strip with the RS down to the RS of the fabric, taking a 5 mm ($\frac{3}{16}$ in) turning on the strip but the full 1.5 cm ($\frac{5}{8}$ in) on the garment. Tack, easing the strips round convex curves, but stretching them round concave ones. End the tacking about 3 cm ($1\frac{1}{4}$ in) from where the join is to come.

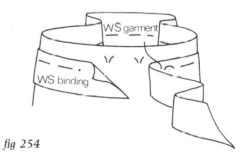

fig 254

Using the iron, press back the ends of the strip on the straight of the grain, and with the folds exactly meeting. Lift the ends and make a seam matching the creases (fig 254). Press open and trim off the ends. Tack across the join.

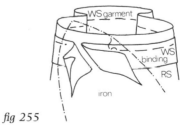

fig 255

Machine in place from the binding side (fig 255).

9   Binding applied to a summer sundress

Trim down all the raw edges but do not cut off too much or the bind will appear limp and unfitted.

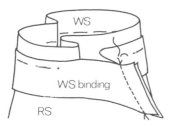

fig 256

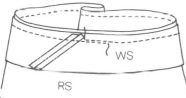

fig 257

On the ws, fold under the raw edge of the binding and then fold the binding over again so that the folded edge falls on the machining (fig 256). Tack and press.

Finish by hemming into every machine stitch.

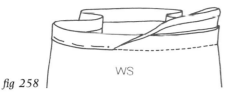

fig 258

Double binding

This can be used where the binding is made from any fine or light-weight material. Try it out first to establish the correct width of strip required, as it cannot be trimmed later.

Cut the strips, fold in half ws together, and press lightly, stretching a little.

Place to the rs of the garment, taking a 1.5 cm

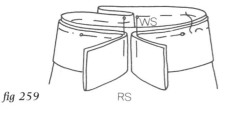

fig 259

($\frac{5}{8}$ in) turning on the garment, but only 5 mm ($\frac{3}{16}$ in) on the binding. Tack to within 6 to 8 cm ($2\frac{1}{2}$ to 3 in) of the end to allow room to make the join (fig 259).

Pin the remainder, and establish where the join is to come. Mark with pins. Trim on the straight grain and make the join (fig 260).

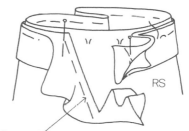

fig 260 denotes seam line on straight of grain

Fold the binding again, then tack and stitch to the garment (fig 261).

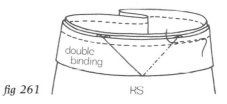

fig 261

Finish by hemming into the machining as for the single binding (fig 262).

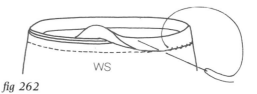

fig 262

Flat binding

There are two main uses for this type of finish to a binding: neatening the raw edge of a coat hem and the facing edges of an unlined coat, and dealing with thick fabrics that would be too bulky if the crossway strip was turned under.

Cut, join and press the crossway strips.

Apply them to the rs and machine. Trim the raw edges carefully (fig 263).

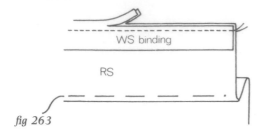

fig 263

Hold the work with the RS towards you ; roll the binding over the edge and, using sewing thread, work with a short prick stitch in the join (fig 264).

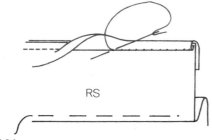

fig 264

This stitching just catches the raw edge of the binding, which lies flat on the WS (fig 265).

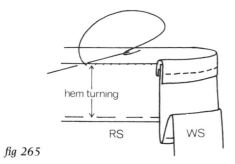

fig 265

Fastenings

Worked buttonholes

Always allow enough time to work all button-holes at one sitting; they will look more even. Make them when the garment is finished.

Dressmaker's buttonholes

Make these on light-weight fabrics where piped buttonholes would be unsuccessful.

Insert a strip of adhesive (eg *Wundaweb*) in addition to the interfacing, between the two layers of fabric, to help prevent fraying. It is not a good idea to try to prevent fraying by overcasting after cutting the slit, as the stitches have to be very shallow, and this usually causes the fabric to fray anyway.

Mark the buttonhole position carefully with lines of tacking (fig 266). The start of the button-hole should be the same distance as the diameter

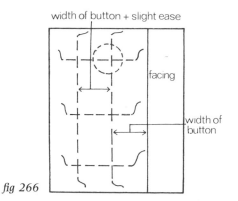

fig 266

of the button in from the finished front edge, other-wise the button will hang over the edge when fastened. Use buttons of a size suitable for the garment (eg small ones on blouses and shirts). If the size and position of the buttonhole is marked

on the pattern, either use the size of button sug-gested, or adjust the position of the buttonholes for your buttons. Allow a little ease; allow more for thick or dome buttons.

Use a suitable thread for the weight of the fabric. On most light-weight fabrics normal sewing thread is best. On heavier fabric use top stitching thread (such as *Drima Bold*), but if it looks clumsy it is better to make piped buttonholes. Use a between needle of a size just big enough to take the thread.

Start with the least visible buttonhole, as you will improve as you go along. Mark each button-hole with a row of small tackings. Push a pin in at one end of the tacking and out at the other, and fold the fabric flat (fig 267).

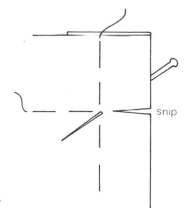

fig 267

Make a small snip at the fold, remove the pin, and snip carefully into the holes left by the pin (fig 268). Remove the remains of the tacks.

Use single thread and start with a knot. Place the knot on the ws a little way from the button-hole, to be cut off later. Begin at the end furthest

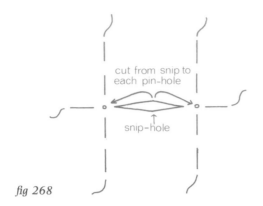

cut from snip to
each pin-hole

↑
snip-hole

fig 268

from the centre front or finished edge, and hold the work with the edge away from you. Work up the left side first.

Bring the thread up level with the end of the cut. Take a small stitch under the raw edge and with the needle still in the fabric, take the double part of the thread near the eye of the needle, winding it first away, then round the needle towards you (fig 269).

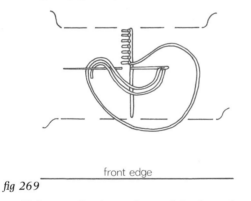

front edge

fig 269

Pull the needle through until the knot forms on the cut edge, then take hold of the thread near to the knot and tug it gently to settle it into position (fig 270).

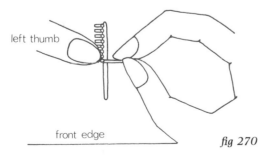

left thumb

front edge

fig 270

Take the next stitch the width of the thread you are using away from the first. Do not work the stitches too close or they will look crowded and uneven, because there will not be enough room for the knots. The knots should just touch, but the uprights should have slight spaces between them. Continue down the first side to the end.

Work round the end of the buttonhole with five stitches arranged evenly, turning the fabric. Keep these stitches shorter than the others for neatness. To prevent the knots from being crowded, lift the thread when settling the knots so that they appear on the top rather than round the raw edge.

Work down the second side.

At the end of the buttonhole take your needle through the first stitch worked so that first and last stitches are joined. Finish the end by making a bar of four stitches, not quite the width of the buttonhole. Pull the thread tight to embed it in the fabric (fig 271). It is important to keep this end neat as it is always visible. Do not make more buttonhole stitches as it looks ugly.

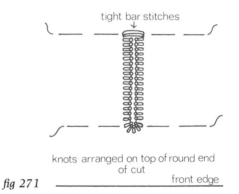

tight bar stitches
↓

knots arranged on top of round end
of cut

fig 271   front edge

Pass the thread to the ws and work loop stitch over the bar stitches to fasten off. Cut off the knot.

Oversew the buttonhole immediately to draw the edges together. Press on both sides when all the buttonholes are complete.

Tailor's buttonholes

These are used on coats and jackets, and it is worth practising until you can do them well as they are a mark of a professional coat.

Gimp is inserted into the edge of the buttonhole for strength and to prevent stretching, and also to produce a raised edge more in keeping with the thickness of the cloth. If you cannot obtain gimp, twist and wax several strands of embroidery thread, or wax just one embroidery thread, although it will not wear as well as tailor's gimp.

Make the buttonholes with silk buttonhole twist or a top-stitching thread (such as *Drima Bold*).

Mark the buttonhole position with sharp chalk, and use a punch to make a hole in the cloth to form the round end. This is to take the thickness of the button shank needed on the heavier fabric. Cut from here to the other end.

Thread the gimp into a gimp needle, or, if this is unobtainable, into a darning needle. Put a knot in the end and bring the gimp out at the end of the buttonhole, starting at the end furthest from the centre front or finished edge. Leave the knot a little way from the buttonhole on the ws.

Thread the buttonhole twist into a large between needle (No. 5 will take the twist) and knot the end. Bring the thread up to the left of the buttonhole holding it with the front edge away from you.

Work buttonhole stitch up the left side, round the end and down the other side. Make the stitches over the gimp, holding the gimp down with the thumb (fig 272). At the end of each side pull the gimp taut to tighten the buttonhole (fig 273).

Remember to lift the knots on the top of the fabric when working the round end and make the stitches very short. Note that the stitch is worked away from you, winding the thread round the needle in the opposite direction from the previous method. This is so that the gimp can be held with the thumb. Pass the gimp through to the ws, and slide the needle between the layers of fabric for a little way. Bring the gimp out and cut off. Cut off the knot.

On the RS work a bar tack across the end of the buttonhole, making four stitches and then stab stitching neatly over them. Fasten off the thread on the ws. Cut off the knot. Oversew the edges and press (fig 274).

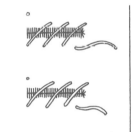

fig 274   oversewn button hole edges

Button snaps

These are available in packs containing several metal button moulds, which you can cover with your own material, and press studs to fit on the back. They are useful on fabrics that are not suitable for buttonholes.

Begin by attaching the knob of the press stud and the button backing plate, one on each side of the upper layer of fabric. Line up the holes in each and attach by stabbing through the holes. Work plenty of stitches to make it look neat.

Attach the well section of the press stud to the under side of the garment using buttonhole stitch.

Cover the button mould by running a gathering thread round a circle of fabric, and snap the button onto the backing plate.

Frogs and ball buttons

These can be made with fabric rouleau, or with round braid or cord. Buy plenty, as you will probably need to experiment.

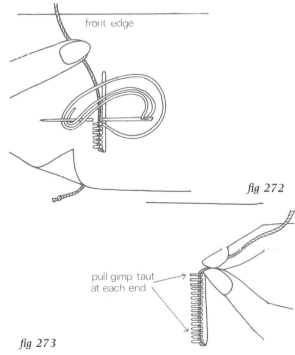

front edge

fig 272

pull gimp taut at each end

fig 273

Frogs

These are usually sewn in pairs on each side of an opening. They are not a firm fastening, and so should not be used on a close fitting garment. A frog usually has three small loops and one larger one to take the button although there are variations. Draw the shape on a piece of tissue paper first (fig 275).

fig 275   design drawn out on paper

Tack the cord to the paper, following the design; the seam of the rouleau should be arranged underneath out of sight. Stitch the centre firmly, then tear the paper away (fig 276).

fig 276   rouleau tacked to design on paper showing direction of loops

Attach the frog with small strong stitches under the cord and then, for added strength, back stitch from the underneath side, feeling the position of the frog.

Ball buttons

Wind the cord following the stages in the diagrams (figs 277, 278, 279, 280), easing the knot loosely to the end when finished.

fig 277

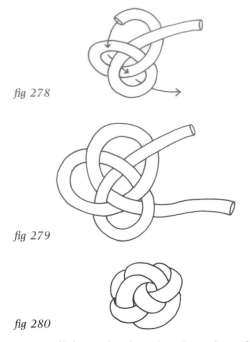

fig 278

fig 279

fig 280

Trim off the ends of cord and stitch to the back of the buttons. If the fabric frays, dab a small spot of contact adhesive (such as *Copydex*) on the ends. Sew the buttons to the garment, taking the stitches through the back of the button, and leaving only a short shank (fig 281).

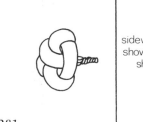

sideways view showing short shank

fig 281

Hooks, eyes and bars

Hooks provide a strong fastening and can be used at points of strain such as the waistband. Use the smallest hook possible if it is likely to be obvious, but use large ones for strength.

Attach the hook by holding it in position a little way back from the edge of the garment. Work about eight strong, deep stitches (but not through to the RS) under the head of the hook, then pass the needle to the loops and hold each loop in

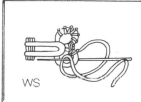

fig 282

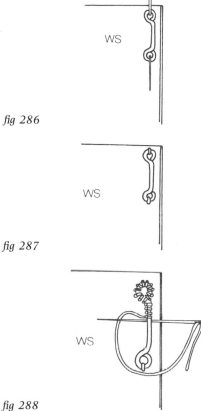

fig 286

position with one oversewing stitch (fig 282).

Finally fill the loops with close buttonhole stitch (fig 283).

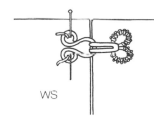

fig 283

If the opening is edge-to-edge, use an eye with the hook, looping it onto the hook and passing a pin through the loops of the eye to hold it in position (fig 284).

fig 287

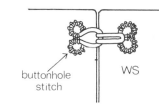

fig 284

Work a single oversewing stitch in each loop, remove the pin and work close buttonhole stitch round each loop (fig 285).

fig 288

can be difficult to fasten, so do not use in places that are awkward to reach. Only cover large bars, as the small ones would be almost impossible to fasten.

A bar made entirely of thread is the least visible of all, but it is not very strong. It is inclined to pull away from the fabric as the stitches all fall in one place. Use only where there is little strain (eg tops of zips).

Make a bar of about four stitches (more for a larger bar) taking the stitches as deep as possible, then work close loop stitches over the entire bar (fig 289).

buttonhole
stitch

fig 285

Use bars wherever possible as they are less visible. Anchor with a pin (fig 286), hold with an oversewing stitch (fig 287), and attach with buttonhole stitch (fig 288).

If the bar is likely to show, cover it completely with loop stitches between the metal loops. These

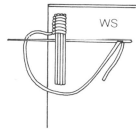

fig 289

If you have to attach a number of hooks to a special garment, you may prefer to partly cover them after sewing them: cut a strip of lining on the cross (or use bought bias binding), press in the edges, and slip it under the heads of the hooks. Hem in place with small stitches (fig 290).

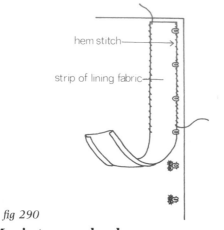

hem stitch

strip of lining fabric

fig 290

Men's trouser hooks

Establish the exact position for a good fit of one or two hooks and bars. Insert the hook at the end of the extension on the left side. First turn in the end of the band and stitch down firmly. Press. Slip a 5 cm (2 in) length of stay tape into the end of the hook and knot like a label on a suitcase. Place the hook in position, and pin the tape at the base of the hook. Sew through the two top eyes of the hook using double waxed thread and plenty of deep oversewing stitches. Sew the base of the hook in the same way, then hem all the edges of the ends of the tape firmly to the interfacing (fig 291).

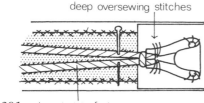

deep oversewing stitches

fig 291    hem to interfacing

To attach the bar, insert a stiletto into the cloth, and slip each end of the bar through. Tie a length of stay tape to each end of the bar and pin down. Oversew each eye of the bar with plenty of strong oversewing stitches. Draw all ends of the tape together at the base, and hem down all tape edges to the interfacing.

Complete the hook end by cutting a piece of silesia, turning in one end and the top edge, and sliding it under the hook. Baste. Turn in the third side and baste. Hem to the waistband. This piece of silesia should cover the extension only and overlap the faced edge by 3 cm ($1\frac{1}{4}$ in). Oversew the raw edge to the waistband (fig 292).

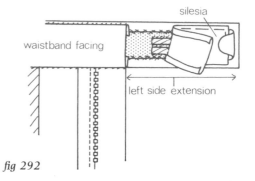

silesia

waistband facing

left side extension

fig 292

If a second hook is required, insert it under the edge of the fly facing, after the left side of the zip has been stitched. This hook will be covered by the waistband backing, which can be of lining or a commercial non-slip variety.

Press studs

Use the smallest size that will be effective, but do not use them at points of strain or movement.

Attach the knob section to the outer part of the garment, and the well section to the underneath. They are less bulky this way and easier to fasten. Use single thread.

Determine the exact position carefully and start the thread with a back stitch (fig 293). Place the

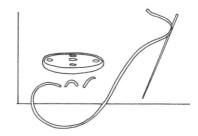

fig 293

press stud over the back stitch and hold it still while you put one oversewing stitch in each hole (fig 294).

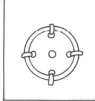

fig 294

The press stud is now anchored in position, and you can attach it permanently by working buttonhole stitch close together to fill each hole. Fasten off beside the press stud or on the ws with a back stitch (fig 295).

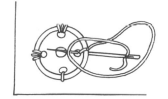

fig 295

Slip a pin through the fabric and through the hole in the centre of the press stud; close up the section of garment and let the point of the pin enter the under part of the garment. Work a back stitch where the pin is, remove the pin, place the press stud over the stitch, and attach it as for the first half.

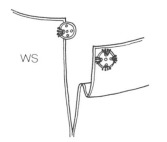

WS

fig 296

At slit necklines, edge-to-edge collars etc, use a transparent plastic press stud and sew the knob section in place close up against the edge of the fabric. Attach the well section to the other part of the garment by stitching through only one hole and allowing the remainder of the press stud to extend beyond the garment (fig 296). When fastened, it brings the opening edge-to-edge.

Covering press studs

This is worth doing on special fabrics and lined garments. Use a piece of lining fabric cut into circles large enough to wrap over the press stud, about twice the diameter. Run a gathering thread round the outer edge of each circle. Make a hole in the centre with a stiletto or large needle (fig 297), and force the knob through it (fig 298). Pull up

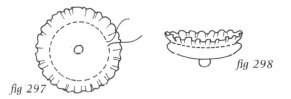

fig 297   *fig 298*

the thread and fasten off. Trim off the raw edges of fabric and press down. Cover the well sections in the same way, but without making a hole; this will occur automatically when the press stud is first fastened. Attach the press studs with buttonhole stitch, using a thread which exactly matches the lining material.

Press studs can be bought attached to tape. Use them in this form if you wish to sew a large number onto a casual or child's garment.

Rouleau loops

These can be used singly or in sets, often with dome-shaped covered buttons.

Soft loops

Cut a crossway strip 2.5 cm (1 in) wide. Allow about 4 cm ($1\frac{1}{2}$ in) for each loop. Press the strips, stretching them slightly. Fold the strip in half with RS together, and tack down the centre. Set the machine to a slight zigzag stitch and machine down the centre. The actual position of the stitching in relation to the folded edge varies with the thickness of the fabric. If you can use the edge of the machine foot as a guide it will help to keep the line straight. Trim down the turnings until they are slightly narrower than the rouleau itself (fig 299). If too much is cut away the loops will be

WS

fig 299

insubstantial and floppy. It is worth practising on a spare strip first to obtain the best width of loop for the fabric and for the button to be used.

Slip an elastic threader, metal bodkin, or special rouleau loop turner into the end of the strip, and firmly sew the eye to the turnings of the fabric (fig 300). Use the ends of the machine thread to

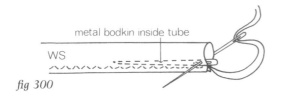

fig 300

do this. Pull the strip RS out by gently easing the fabric back over the attached end (fig 301). Once started, it will pull through easily. Cut off the ends; do not press.

fig 301

To make single loops, cut up the rouleau and place each loop against the fitting line with the loop itself extending back into the garment. Experiment with the size by fastening it over the button. Loops tend to stretch in wear, so make it a tight fit. Tack the ends in place, and machine across on the fitting line of the garment.

If making a continuous row of close loops, do not cut the rouleau, but wind it serpentine fashion to form the loops. Tack and machine. If the position of the loops is not marked on the pattern, cut a piece of tissue paper the length of the loop section, fold into four or six or however many loops are to be made, tack the loops to this, and then tack the paper to the garment. Tear off the paper after machining across the loops (fig 302).

Place the facing (or other edge finish, such as binding) on top of the loops RS down. Machine in place from the garment side, making sure you stitch exactly on top of the machining holding the loops in place, or even slightly to one side, to prevent it from showing later. Trim all the edges, and roll the facing to the WS, so allowing the loops to extend. Tack and press the edge, but not the loops.

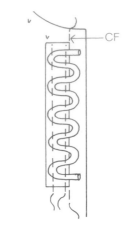

fig 302

Corded loops

These are more substantial than soft loops; they do not stretch, and they look more professional on outer garments.

Cut crossway strips, join and stretch. Cut a piece of thin, pre-shrunk piping cord twice the length of the strip, and wrap the strip round the cord, WS out, but start with end at the centre of the cord. Using the piping foot, machine across the end of the cord to hold it, and then stitch close to the cord down the remaining length of the strip (fig 303).

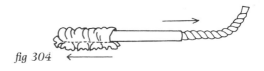

fig 303

Pull the cord, and ease the fabric over it. Cut off the surplus cord to use another time (fig 304). Attach the loops as described for 'soft loops', above.

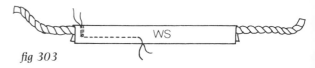

fig 304

Rouleau bows

Make lengths of rouleau, and insert the ends in a seam if possible, or make the tie ends a continuation of a binding (eg as a finish on a long gathered sleeve). To finish the ends of the rouleau (fig 305),

fig 305

push the raw edges back into the tube using a bodkin (figs 306, 307).

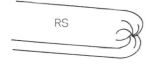

fig 306 pushing in raw ends

fig 307 end tucked in

Rouleau decoration

To make an open lattice decoration, make plenty of rouleau, and press it flat with the seam along one side. Take the section of pattern to be latticed and cut it out again in paper, but cutting the whole section (fig 308).

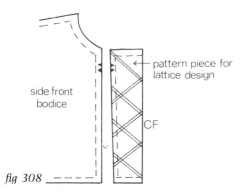

fig 308

Rule lines on the paper (or use squared pattern paper) and tack the rouleau to it. Tack this to the rest of the garment and stitch (fig 309).

Binding is a good finish on an outside edge such as a neckline or an armhole. Machine, and tear away the paper, then finish off the seam, binding etc.

To make close lattice, as for a patch pocket, interweave the rouleau, lay the pattern on, and

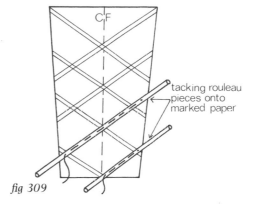

fig 309

cut out. Bind the edges or stitch round to hold before turning in the edges.

Pointed edging

Place the rouleau on the RS of the garment and machine, folding into points, first out, then across, then towards you (fig 310). Place the facing on

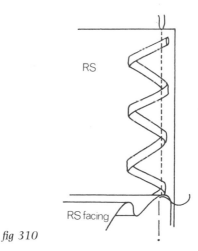

fig 310

top, RS down, and stitch. When the facing is rolled over, the edging appears. The width of the rouleau determines the size of the points. This edging can also be made with petersham ribbon.

Open pointed edging

Finish the garment edge with facing, binding etc, then mark points about 2 cm ($\frac{3}{4}$ in) apart. Attach the rouleau at these points by hand, allowing it to extend from there, then fold it back to meet the next mark, and so on (fig 311).

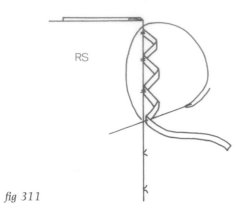

fig 311

Eyelets

If these are for decoration through a single or double layer of woven fabric, they can be made by pushing a stiletto into the fabric, twisting it, and then quickly working a close neat oversewing stitch all round (fig 312). The stitching can be in a contrasting colour.

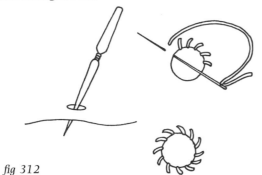

fig 312

If the eyelets are in a belt, then an actual hole must be punched with a buttonhole punch. Work buttonhole stitch round the hole to neaten the raw edge and take the wear of the prong.

Belts

Fabric belts

Decide how the belt is to be fastened as this affects the amount of overlap needed. If fastening at the side under the arm, allow 4 cm (1½ in), and fasten with hooks. To fasten with a touch fastener (such as *Velcro*) allow 7 cm (2¾ in). If attaching a buckle, allow 10 cm (4 in). If it is a clasp, allow 3 cm (1¼ in) at each end.

Cut a waist length plus overlap of pelmet-weight *Vilene*, belt stiffening or petersham.

Straight belt

Cut a length of fabric on the straight grain (or on the cross for special effect), longer than the stiffening and twice the width plus turnings (fig 313).

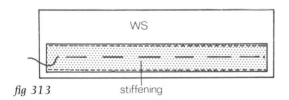

fig 313 stiffening

Place the stiffening 1 cm (⅜ in) from the edge on the ws and tack. Either machine along each edge or herringbone. Fold over the 1 cm (⅜ in) turning and tack. Turn in the ends, fold the fabric

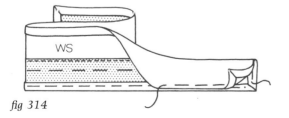

fig 314

over to cover the second side of the belt, and turn in the raw edge so that it is slightly back from the edge. Tack (fig 314). Slip hem the ends, and hem the long edge. Press.

Straight belt with picot edge

Cover one side of the stiffening with fabric, and tack. Turn all raw edges over to the ws of the belt and tack (fig 315). Press.

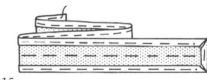

fig 315

Place coloured or white petersham ribbon, a little wider than the belt, to the ws and tack (fig 316), turning a narrow hem to the ws at the end. Machine all round (fig 317).

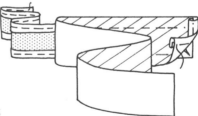

fig 316

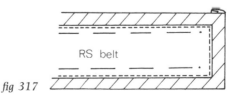

fig 317 RS belt

Curved belt

Use a length of curved petersham, or if you want a wider belt cut a piece of pelmet *Vilene*, using the petersham as a guide. Remember to allow the overlap.

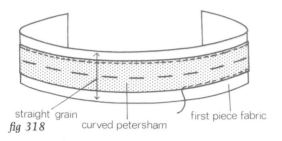

straight grain curved petersham first piece fabric

fig 318

Place the stiffening on a double layer of fabric with the straight grain at the centre of the belt. Cut out round the stiffening allowing turnings all round. Tack one piece of fabric to the stiffening and machine along both edges (fig 318). Place the second piece of fabric against the first, RS together, and tack along the upper, concave edge. Machine just off the edge of the stiffening (fig 319). Run the iron along the join between the two layers of fabric. Turn up the fabric along the lower edge and tack. Turn in the ends and tack.

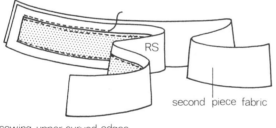

RS

second piece fabric

sewing upper curved edges
through both fabric pieces　　　　*fig 319*

Fold the second piece of fabric over to cover the belt, and turn in the outside edge so that it falls just back from the edge of the belt. As this is curved, it helps to pin it vertically at intervals before tacking. Press; hem along all three edges (fig 320).

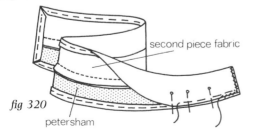

second piece fabric

fig 320

petersham

Tie belt

Cut a length of fabric on the straight grain twice the width required plus two turnings, allow as much length as you want for tying in a knot or a bow. Soft fabrics can be interfaced with soft *Vilene*.

If the fabric has to be joined, make the join on the cross as it 'gives', and is less bulky and less obvious (figs 321, 322, 323).

Fold the fabric with RS together and tack. Angle the ends of the belt if you wish. Chalk a line on which to stitch. Machine across each end and almost to the centre, leaving a gap for turning through. Do not have the gap where there is a join. Press the stitching flat.

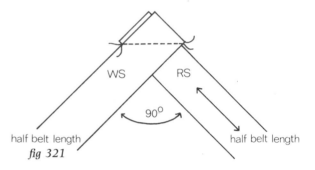

WS　　RS

90°

half belt length　　　　　　half belt length

fig 321

Trim all edges and cut off corners.

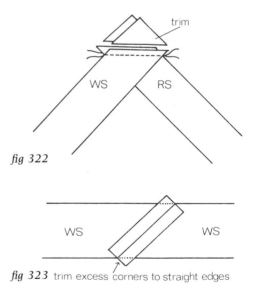

trim

WS　　RS

fig 322

WS　　　　　　WS

fig 323　trim excess corners to straight edges

Turn through with a ruler or a knitting needle. Pull out the corners well and roll the edge and tack. Turn in the raw edges at the gap and tack. Press well. Slip stitch the gap. Remove tacks.

A variety of other tie belts can be made with rouleau either single or plaited.

Belt loops

Thread loops

Always work through a double thickness of fabric. If a loop has to be made where there is no seam then place a length of seam binding on the ws to provide the second layer.

Use a long piece of thread, doubled and waxed. Place the belt in position and pin. Bring the needle up at one side of the belt, over and down into the fabric the other side (fig 324).

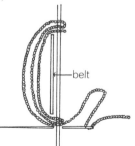

fig 324

Bring the needle up again very close and pass it over the top of the belt. Make four strands in this way (fig 325).

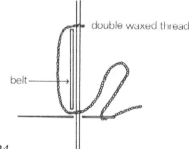

fig 325

Remove the belt. Work close loop stitch across the threads (fig 326).

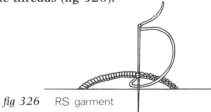

fig 326   RS garment

An alternative method is to work chain stitch over the belt. This makes a finer loop but the ends are weak and liable to pull the fabric.

Fabric loops

Straight loops for belts and trousers can be made from a length of fabric 1.5 cm ($\frac{5}{8}$ in) wide. Make one long piece and cut it up afterwards. Turn in 5 mm ($\frac{3}{16}$ in) each side of the strip and press (fig 327). Fold so that the edges meet, and tack. Press. Machine along both edges (fig 328).

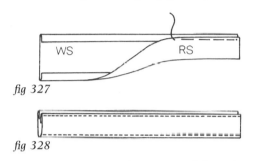

fig 327

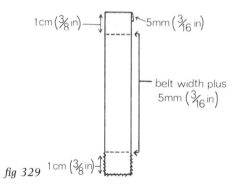

fig 328

Cut it into pieces the required lengths, ie the width of the belt plus 5 mm ($\frac{3}{16}$ in) ease, plus 1.5 cm ($\frac{5}{8}$ in) at each end to stitch down. Turn in 5 mm ($\frac{3}{16}$ in) at each end and place the loop in position. Hem round the end and back stitch across the loop 5 mm ($\frac{3}{16}$ in) in from the end. On some fabrics it will look good to machine these ends (fig 329).

fig 329

If attaching to trousers, insert the upper ends of the loops into the top join of the waistband, then bring the other end down and stitch.

Crossway loops can be made from a long length of crossway fabric 1.5 cm ($\frac{5}{8}$ in) wide, folded and machined as for rouleau loops. Turn through and cut into lengths. Place the belt in position and pin, snip the seam on either side of the belt and push the ends of the loop in. Remove the belt, turn to the ws and stitch up the seams catching in the ends of the loops.

Fastening a belt

A buckle with prong and eyelets is adjustable, but clasps or prongless buckles are not, so it is advisable to make at least one end adjustable with *Velcro*. Allow for this when calculating the length of the belt; you will need at least 4 cm ($1\frac{1}{2}$ in) of overlap. Pass the end of the belt over the buckle or clasp, hem one side of *Velcro* to the overlap and the other to the back of the belt (fig 330).

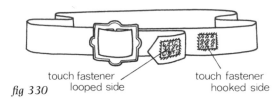

touch fastener
looped side

touch fastener
hooked side

fig 330

Finishing Touches

Coat hangers

Either make a tube of rouleau from lining 8 cm ($3\frac{1}{8}$ in) long cut on the cross and insert the ends under the lining at the neckline, or make a stronger hanger by folding an 8 cm ($3\frac{1}{8}$ in) length of straight grain lining. Fold in each edge, fold again to a finished width of 5 mm ($\frac{3}{16}$ in). Tack and press. Slip stitch the folded edges together (fig 331).

Turn in each end and hem in position, back stitching firmly across the end to form a square of stitching. This hanger should be stitched close up against the edge of the lining at the back of the neck (fig 332).

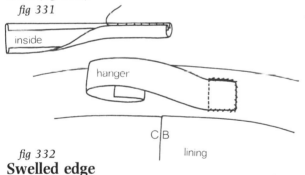

fig 331

fig 332

Swelled edge

This is formed by working prick stitch around the finished, pressed edges of collars, lapels and pocket flaps. Work with the RS towards you; on light fabrics the stitches should be 3 mm ($\frac{1}{8}$ in) from the edge, on heavier fabrics a little more. Use a small needle. (See page 11 for prick stitch.)

On a lapel, work on the RS of the jacket up to the turn of the lapel, and then change over so that you stitch from the RS on the lapel and collar.

If the cloth is very bulky, work it by stabbing through from side to side.

Saddle stitching

This is a decorative top stitching, worked by hand, after the garment is complete. Use top stitching thread, buttonhole twist, fine embroidery cotton or other thick yarn, threaded into a needle with an eye large enough to take the thread. It is fairly easy to saddle stitch a woven fabric, especially a soft woollen one, but it is more difficult to pass the thread through a synthetic knit, and you may have to be satisfied with a smaller needle and therefore a finer thread on some fabrics. Try it out before working directly on the garment.

Work from right to left, if right handed, on the RS of the garment. It is easier to keep even and produces a more raised stitch if you work a back stitch rather than a forward running stitch. Bring the thread out and take the needle just over half-way back to the previous stitch, taking the needle under again and emerging an even distance further on (fig 333). Keep the stitching small, big stitches look amateurish, and keep the stitches slightly longer than the gaps between (fig 334). Do not try

arrowheads show direction of stitch

cross-section of stitch used on two layers of fabric
fig 333   to produce saddle-stitch

fig 334

to take the needle through to the ws, or the back of the garment will look untidy.

Do not use saddle stitching as a means of holding an edge or a facing back. This should have been done earlier as part of the construction, either by holding down with fabric adhesive strip (such as *Wundaweb*), or by working a swelled edge finish (see page 103). The latter will have the advantage of giving you a line on which to saddle stitch.

If it is essential for the stitching to show on both the RS and the WS it would be best to do machine top stitching (see page 106), but with top stitching thread on the spool as well as on the top of the machine.

Braids and lace

Ric-rac braid

Flat

Mark the position with chalk, lay the braid on the line and hold it while stitching. Work a tiny prick stitch in each point of the braid criss-crossing the thread on the WS as you move from one point to the next (fig 335).

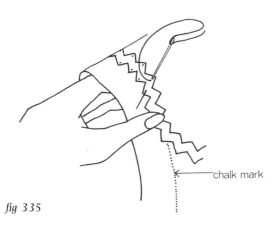

fig 335

The alternative is to work a row of back stitching or machining down the centre of the braid, but with this method the points of the braid will tend to curl up.

Ric-rac can be attached decoratively by working herringbone stitch across the braid, using a contrasting embroidery thread (fig 336).

fig 336

Edging

This produces a picot edge. Place the ric-rac to the RS of the garment with the centre of the braid over the fitting line. Tack down the centre (fig 337).

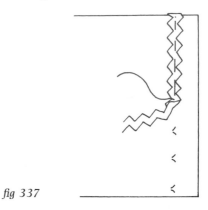

fig 337

Place facing RS down onto the braid. Turn the work over and tack, following the fitting line exactly. Machine on this line. Trim the turnings, but do not cut the ric-rac. Roll and finish the facings in the usual way (fig 338).

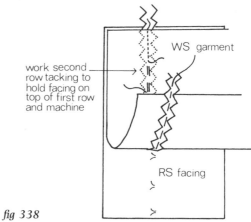

work second row tacking to hold facing on top of first row and machine

WS garment

RS facing

fig 338

Raised braid

Most raised braids look best attached by hand. Catch it down lightly with one prick stitch or fell stitch (depending on the design of the braid) in each extending bead along the edge of the braid.

Soutache

This is a narrow two-cord silky braid designed to be sewn down the centre. This is best done with a hand prick stitch but it can be done by machine using the zip foot.

Fancy braid

This is the kind of braid which is used on men's dinner jacket trousers. Attach it by hand using felling down each edge. Do not pull the thread tightly.

Folded braid

For greatest accuracy attach both sides of folded braid, or wide two-colour braid, with felling, after tacking in place first. This braid can also be attached by machining the first side, then folding the braid over and felling the second side. These braids are soft and often woven on the bias, and so will go easily round curves, but because of this movement they must be tacked first.

Take care to press all braids on the ws only, on a towel. If the ends of the braid come at a seam, a neat finish is to make a small slit in the seam and push the ends of the braid through, re-stitching the seam afterwards.

Maribou trimming

Make a series of big bar tacks about 10 cm (4 in) apart on the RS of the garment and thread the maribou through (fig 339). This makes it easy to remove, particularly to dry clean the garment, and also (as the trim is expensive) in order to use it again.

fig 339

Lace edging

Lay the edge of the lace over the fabric and hem

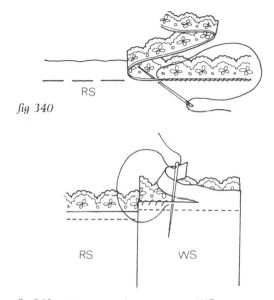

fig 340

fig 341   trimming and neatening on WS

(fig 340), trimming and neatening the fabric raw edge underneath (fig 341), or turn a narrow hem on the fabric and hem or machine it before putting the edge of the lace to it, then oversew or whip it in place.

Lace insertion

Place the lace in position and tack. Stitch both edges by hand or machine (fig 342). Trim away the fabric on the ws and neaten with hand-overcasting (fig 343).

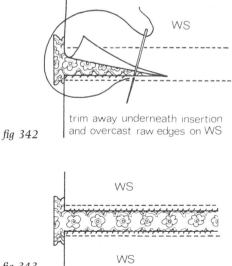

fig 342   trim away underneath insertion and overcast raw edges on WS

fig 343

Lace appliqué

Place the motif in position (fig 344), slip a small piece of fabric adhesive (such as *Wundaweb*) underneath, and press using a damp muslin. Attach round the edge with oversewing or loop stitch in a thread exactly matching the lace (fig 345). If you wish to trim fabric away on the ws for an open effect, you cannot use adhesive (fig 346).

motif basted in position

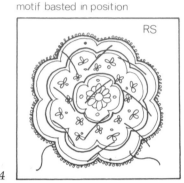

fig 344

loop stitching edge of motif to garment

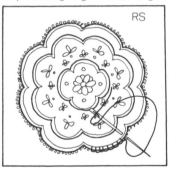

fig 345

trim away on WS garment the fabric below motif and overcast raw edges

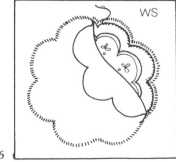

fig 346

Joining lace

To join lace, overlap the two ends, and work close oversewing stitches across the width of the lace (fig 347), following the outline of part of the design. Trim away the excess lace close to the stitching on both the rs and the ws (fig 348).

fig 347

trim away at back

fig 348   trim ends close to oversewing

To mitre a corner mark the angle of the mitre on each end of lace, and overlap the two ends, matching the tack marks. Oversew closely round a main part of the design. Trim away the surplus lace on the rs and the ws.

To press the lace place the rs down onto a folded towel; press lightly with a steam iron.

Top stitching

This is easier to keep even if worked through only two layers of fabric and not, as often suggested, by pressing both seam turnings to one side, and therefore stitching through three layers. The more layers of fabric there are, the more inclined the machining will be to wobble or look uneven so where possible work the top stitching early on in the construction of the garment. If you want a raised effect place a crossway strip of lawn or a length of bias binding on the ws under the seam turning.

Insert a number 110 (18) machine needle and thread the top of the machine with a top stitching thread (such as *Drima Bold*); use a normal thread underneath. Set the machine to a fairly large stitch, or one that looks correct on your fabric. Stitch from the rs using the edge or groove in the foot as a guide. Pivot carefully at the corners, and when going round curves turn the wheel of the machine by hand to proceed stitch by stitch.

In places where you have no choice but to work

the top stitching last, for example round a collar or front edges, remember that it is very important to trim the turnings right down within the edge to reduce the number of layers you stitch through.

Top stitching can also be worked effectively on modern machines by using two reels of normal thread on the top of the machine (one on each spindle) and then have both threads following the same path to the needle. Use the spool below in the usual way. Machine from the right side with a long stitch.

It is also very effective to use the double needle on the machine and work two close rows of top stitching at once. Use two reels of normal sewing thread on the top of the machine.

Fringes

A fringe can be made from lengths of cut wool, or from strands taken from the fabric; fringing can be bought ready made up. A long silky fringe looks more luxurious if a double row is applied.

Fringe in a seam
Lay lengths of yarn on the RS of the fabric, and place the other piece of fabric RS down. Tack and machine. Work two rows of stitching to prevent the fringe from falling out. Fold the fabric over and tack and press. Trim the fringe.

Knotted fringe
Apply this to a finished edge; it is usually only successful on woven fabrics where a hole is easily made between the threads (fig 349). Use a small

fig 349

crochet hook to pass bundles of yarns through the edge of the fabric (fig 350). Pull the ends of the yarn through the loop (fig 351) and pull the knot tight (fig 352).

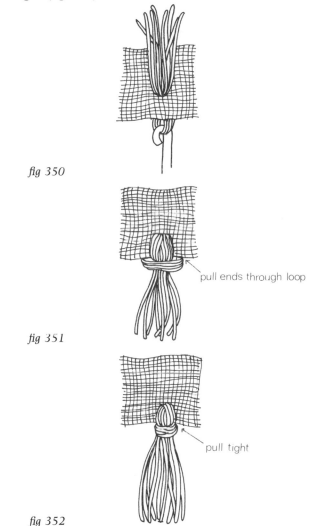

fig 350

fig 351

pull ends through loop

fig 352

pull tight

Fringed fabric
Woven fabrics can be unravelled to produce a fringe. Prevent further unravelling by working a small zigzag stitch over the edge in a perfectly matching thread.

Loop stitch finish

A hand finish that becomes popular from time to time is a loop stitched edge. It can be worked over a raw edge on some fabrics such as tweed or jersey, but on others turn and finish a hem in the usual way first.

Use contrasting thick thread or wool, hold the edge towards you, and work from left to right. Make sure the yarn is washable if the garment is to be washed. The stitches should form squares (fig 353) and can be any size from 5 mm ($\frac{3}{16}$ in) to 1 cm ($\frac{3}{8}$ in).

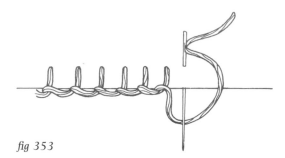

fig 353

Shirring with elastic thread

The number of rows worked will depend on how tight the area needs to be. The more rows of shirring worked the tighter it becomes. Three or four rows will often be enough on a sleeve, but at least ten or twelve rows will be needed for a bodice or a flat area of shirring. Always machine on the RS of the fabric.

First method

Wind the elastic onto the machine spool using the spool-winding mechanism on the machine. This ensures that the elastic is wound under tension; it is not possible to maintain an even tension when winding by hand. Thread the machine with a synthetic thread on top and the elastic underneath. Adjust the machine to the largest straight stitch it will do. Work a row of stitching. This row will barely produce gathering. Work a second row about 1 cm ($\frac{3}{8}$ in) or the width of part of the foot away, smoothing out the fabric. Work as many subsequent rows as are necessary.

Second method

Put the embroidery foot on the machine and thread the end of the elastic through the hole in the foot and pass it to the back. Thread the machine up with synthetic thread. Set the machine to a medium zigzag, about number 2, and a medium length stitch. Work rows of machining, pulling the

elastic as you stitch. The more you pull the more it will gather. You may need to practice just to see how much it needs pulling. Use the foot as a guide for keeping the rows parallel and smooth out the fabric.

Whichever method you are using, fasten off all ends of thread and elastic on the ws by using the thread to hold the elastic down. Where possible, work shirring across the whole width of a section so that the ends will be caught in a seam later, otherwise the shirring will be weak and will not last very long. Even when it is caught in a seam it is a wise precaution to double stitch across the shirring when stitching the seam.

To complete the work, pass the shirred area through the steam from a kettle of boiling water. This will shrink the elastic and draw it up tighter.

Gauging

Gauging is visible gathering, used as decoration, usually in short sections.

Work several parallel rows of large machining, using synthetic thread (such as Coats' *Drima*) for strength. The distance between the rows will depend upon the thickness and design of the fabric and the size of the area of gauging. Work all rows of stitching, pin each end to the section to be attached, pull up the threads by grasping all the spool thread ends together. Fasten off all the ends by sewing them in on the ws. To prevent stretching or breaking, cut a piece of fabric or lining material the length of the gauged section plus turnings, hem the top and bottom edges, turn in the two ends and place ws down onto the back of the gauging. Hem in place across the two ends.

Cord gathering

Cord gathering is decorative gathering using a pearlcord or crochet cotton and a zigzag stitch.

Fix the embroidery foot on the machine and thread the cord through the hole in the foot. Set the machine to a medium zigzag, about number 2, and a fairly long stitch. Machine on the RS and work two rows or more of stitching 2 cm ($\frac{3}{4}$ in) apart. Take hold of all the ends of the cord together and pull up to size. If the gathers extend for the full width of a garment section the ends of the thread will be caught and held in a seam later, but if not, then the ends of the thread and the cord must be passed to the ws and sewn in.

Decorative facing

This is a shaped facing finished on the RS for effect. It can be in contrasting plain or print fabric and it can have a different texture from the garment fabric.

The edge to be attached first must be cut the same shape as the garment edge. The outer edge of the facing can be parallel or it can be shaped. It is best not to interface this type of edging, even if it is a neck edge, as it makes the facing difficult to handle. If, however, the fabric is particularly soft or floppy, attach a narrow strip of iron-on interfacing to the garment on the RS (fig 354).

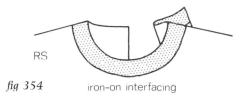

fig 354 iron-on interfacing

Attach the facing pieces by tacking with the RS facing to the ws of the garment. Make the joins in the facing by pressing over the raw edges so that the folds meet (fig 355), then lift the ends and

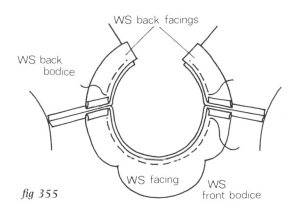

fig 355

make a join on the crease (fig 356). Trim the raw edges and press them open.

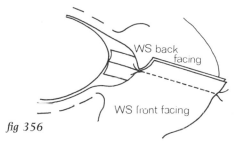

fig 356

Machine the facing to the garment, trim and layer the turnings, and roll the facing to the RS (fig 357).

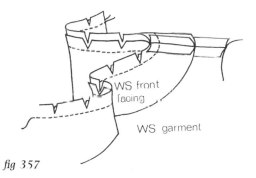

fig 357

Roll and tack the edge, keeping the join slightly to the ws of the garment. Press well. Lay the facing flat onto the RS of the garment and work a row of basting to hold (fig 358).

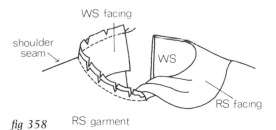

fig 358 RS garment

Run a row of tacking on the outer edge of the facing on the fitting line, exactly where the finished edge is to be; this may be parallel with the garment edge or it may be scalloped, or it may be of a more intricate shape. Trim down the raw edge so that only about 4 mm ($\frac{1}{8}$ in) of raw edge extends beyond the tacking (fig 359).

Turn under and tack this edge and press. If there are corners to be worked, as, for example, on a square neck, it will help to mitre the corners and slip stitch them together.

10   *Decorative facing applied to the neckline and sleeves*

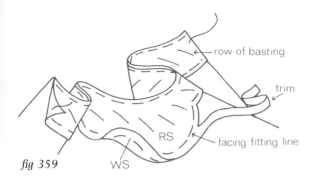

fig 359

with a row of machining on the edge, or, using an easier method, hold down with a small hand slip stitch (fig 360). Remove all tacks and press.

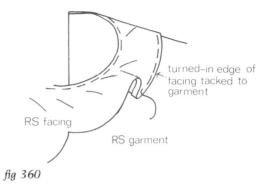

Tack the edge down onto the garment and finish

fig 360

List of Suppliers

T. Beazley & Sons Ltd
23 Ganton Street
Regent Street
London W1
Tailoring supplies and mail order

Bernina Sewing Centre
10 Wardour Street
London W1
Bernina sewing machines

John Lewis & Co Ltd
Oxford Street
London W1A 1EX
Haberdashery and fabrics and mail order

The Needlewoman Shop
146 Regent Street
London W1
Haberdashery, fabrics and mail order

Singer Co Ltd
255 High Street
Guildford
Surrey
List of sewing machine stockists available

Vilene Ltd
PO Box 3
Greetland
Halifax
Yorkshire
List of stockists of Vilene products available

Index

Belts
    fabric 99–101
    fastening 102
    loops 101–2
Binding
    crossway and bias strips 84–5
    double 87
    flat 87–8
    single 85, 87
Braid 104–5

Coat hangers 103
Collars
    semi-tailored coat or dress 66–8
    shirt 68–9
    tailored coat or jacket 62–6
Cord gathering 108–9
Cuffs
    dress 74–5
    hole-and-button 77, 79
    shirt 75–7
    wrap 74

Darts 14
Decorative facing 109–11

Facings, combined 33–4
Fastenings
    bars 93
    button snaps 91
    eyelets 98
    eyes 93
    frogs and ball buttons 91–2
    hooks, 92, 93, 94
    press studs 94–5
    rouleau loops 95–8
Fringes 107

Gauging 108

Hems
    coat 82–3
    circular 81–2
    curved 81
    narrow 80
    reinforcing 83
    wide straight 81

Interfacing
    back neck 32–3
    coat or jacket 30–2
    combined facings 33–4

Lace 105–6
Linings
    coat or jacket 45–7
    loose 43–5
    sleeve 47–8
Loop stitch finish 107–8

Mounting 49

Pleats
    box 17
    inverted 16–17
    knife 15–16
Pockets
    flap 21–2
    flap and jetted 25–6
    inside breast 25
    jetted 22–5
    men's trouser side-seam 28–9
    patch 20–1
    seam 28
    trouser back 25
    welt 26–8
Pressing equipment 12

Saddle stitching 103–4
Seams
    angled 35
    coat shoulder 39
    corded 35–6
    machine fell 37
    piped 37, 39
    slot 39–40
    trouser, reinforced 41
    welt 40
Shirring with elastic thread 108
Shoulders
    pads 50
    sleeve head roll 51
Sleeve openings
    continuous strip 71–2
    faced slit 71
    gap-in-sleeve 70
    hemmed 70–1
    man's shirt 72–3
    seam 70
    shirt 72
Swelled edge 103

Tailoring terms 9–12
Top-stitching 106–7
Trouser creases 42

Waistlines
    man's trouser waistband 58–9
    stay 61
    waistband backing 61

Zip openings
    inserting a zip fastener 52–5,
       56, 59–60
    man's trouser zip 55–6